DRAMA CLASSICS

The Drama Classics series aims to offer the world's greatest plays in affordable paperback editions for students, actors and theatregoers. The hallmarks of the series are accessible introductions, uncluttered texts and an overall theatrical perspective.

Given that readers may be encountering a particular play for the first time, the introduction seeks to fill in the theatrical/historical background and to outline the chief themes rather than concentrate on interpretational and textual analysis. Similarly the play-texts themselves are free of footnotes and other interpolations: instead there is an end-glossary of 'difficult' words and phrases.

The texts of the English-language plays in the series have been prepared taking full account of all existing scholarship. The foreign-language plays have been newly translated into a modern English that is both actable and accurate: many of the translators regularly have their work staged professionally.

Edited until his early death by Kenneth McLeish, the Drama Classics series continues with his aim of providing a first-class library of dramatic literature representing the best of world theatre.

Associate editors:
Professor Trevor R. Griffiths
Dr. Colin Counsell
School of Arts and Humanities
University of North London

DRAMA CLASSICS *the first hundred*

The publishers welcome suggestions for further titles

DRAMA CLASSICS

THE CHANGELING

by

Thomas Middleton
and
William Rowley

edited and introduced by
Trevor R. Griffiths

NICK HERN BOOKS

London

www.nickhernbooks.co.uk

A Drama Classic

This edition of *The Changeling* first published in Great Britain
as a paperback original in 2000 by Nick Hern Books Limited,
14 Larden Road, London W3 7ST

Copyright in the introduction © Nick Hern Books, 2000

Copyright in this edition of the text
© Trevor R. Griffiths, 2000

Typeset by Country Setting, Kingsdown, Kent CT14 8ES
Printed by Athenaeum Press, Gateshead, Tyne and Wear

A CIP catalogue record for this book is available from
the British Library

ISBN 1 85459 192 4

Introduction

The Authors

The Changeling (1622) was written jointly by Thomas Middleton (1580-1627) and William Rowley (?1585-1626).

Middleton, the son of a wealthy bricklayer, attended Oxford University but left without obtaining a degree. By 1601 he was in London 'daily accompanying the players' and became one of Philip Henslowe's stable of playwrights collaborating with Thomas Dekker, Michael Drayton and Anthony Munday on various plays that have not survived. He wrote plays with Dekker for the companies of boys performing at Blackfriars and Paul's, for Prince Charles's company, for Lady Elizabeth's Men and after 1615 for the King's Men. He also wrote civic and Lord Mayor's pageants, becoming Chronologer to the City of London in 1620. His 1624 play *A Game at Chess* achieved the longest run of any Jacobean play (nine days), but ran foul of the authorities for its topical satire against Spain. His plays include the comedies *A Mad World, My Masters* (1604?), *The Roaring Girl* (with Dekker, 1610?) and *A Chaste Maid in Cheapside* (1611) and the tragedy *Women Beware Women* (1621). He is now also widely regarded as the author of *The Revenger's Tragedy* (1606) traditionally ascribed to Cyril Tourneur.

Rowley was a leading comic actor with the Duke of York's Men (which became Prince Charles's company) and then the King's Men. His parts included the clown in his own *All's Lost by Lust* (1622) and the fat bishop in *A Game at Chess*. As a dramatist he collaborated with Thomas Heywood, Dekker, Ford, Fletcher, and Webster as well as with Middleton, with whom he wrote both *A Fair Quarrel* (1615?) and *The Changeling*. It is generally agreed that Rowley wrote the subplot and the opening and closing scenes of *The Changeling*, which suggests that the authors' relationship was a genuine collaboration, rather than, as has sometimes been suggested, a master/servant relationship, with Middleton as the senior partner taking responsibility for the tragic parts while leaving his junior to get on with comic relief.

What Happens in the Play

Beatrice-Joanna, the daughter of Vermandero, is betrothed to Alonzo De Piraquo.

1.1 Alsemero has fallen in love with Beatrice-Joanna, not knowing she is engaged. Beatrice-Joanna reciprocates his feelings. Vermandero's servant De Flores (who is infatuated with her) informs Beatrice-Joanna of her father's arrival but she treats him with scorn. Vermandero welcomes Alsemero and tells him of the forthcoming marriage. Alsemero decides to leave when he finds out that Beatrice-Joanna is engaged, but Vermandero persuades him to stay.

1.2 Alibius, who runs a madhouse, and his servant Lollio discuss arrangements for protecting Alibius's young wife Isabella from sexual temptation. They welcome a new patient, Antonio, who is actually a nobleman disguised as a fool in order to attempt to seduce Isabella.

2.1 Beatrice-Joanna is trying to find a way to marry Alsemero rather than Alonzo. She and De Flores quarrel again. Alonzo's brother Tomazo suspects that Beatrice-Joanna's affections for Alonzo have cooled.

2. 2 Unknown to Alsemero, Beatrice-Joanna decides to use De Flores to kill Alonzo. De Flores, delighted by Beatrice-Joanna's changed attitude towards him, arranges to show Alonzo the castle, in order to murder him.

3.1–2 De Flores kills Alonzo and decides to give Beatrice-Joanna Alonzo's ring. He has to cut off Alonzo's finger because he cannot get his ring off by itself.

3.3 Lollio introduces Isabella to the madman Franciscus, a new inmate who is actually another noblemen and would-be seducer. Antonio, overheard by Lollio, tells Isabella that he is actually her would-be lover, not a fool.

3.4 De Flores tells Beatrice-Joanna that Alonzo is dead and shows her the finger. As she begins to realise the full horror of what she has done, he tells her that she, not money, will be his reward.

4.1 In a dumb show, Vermandero puzzles over Alonzo's apparent flight but permits Alsemero to become betrothed to Beatrice-Joanna. Beatrice-Joanna discovers that Alsemero has a virginity testing kit. Worried that he will discover that she has lost her virginity (to De Flores), she tests Diaphanta, her confidante, before allowing her to take her own place in the bridal bed.

4.2 Vermandero discovers that Franciscus and Antonio are absent and quarrels with Tomazo, Alonzo's brother, who is accusing him of having a part in Alonzo's death. Jasperino, Alsemero's friend, has overheard a compromising encounter between De Flores and Beatrice-Joanna. This leads Alsemero to test Beatrice-Joanna with his virginity potion. She, having already tested it on Diaphanta, is able to fake the necessary reactions, thus convincing Alsemero of her chastity.

4.3 Isabella tells Lollio that she has two disguised suitors. She then pretends to be a madwoman in order to test Antonio, who finds her repulsive in disguise. Lollio confronts Franciscus.

5.1 Beatrice-Joanna is worried because Diaphanta is still in the bridal bed. De Flores sets fire to Diaphanta's bedroom in order to rouse the house. In the confusion, he shoots her to ensure her silence.

5.2 Vermandero tells Tomazo that Alibius and Isabella have confirmed his suspicions of Franciscus and Antonio.

5.3 Alsemero and Jasperino are now convinced that Beatrice-Joanna is guilty of adultery with De Flores. She explains her conduct, admitting her role in Alonzo's death, and Alsemero locks her and De Flores together in a closet. When Vermandero comes to explain his version of Alonzo's death, Alsemero tells him the truth and reveals De Flores and Beatrice-Joanna, both now fatally wounded at De Flores' hand.

Contexts

The earliest known performance of *The Changeling* took place at Court in 1624 and it was licensed to the Phoenix, an indoor playhouse. Its early performances would, then, have taken place indoors, in an environment lit by artificial lighting, rather than in one of the familiar open-air amphitheatres, such as the Globe. Although the indoor playhouses were smaller than the amphitheatres, the audience still largely shared the same space as the actors and the claustrophobic atmosphere of *The Changeling* may well have been enhanced by the relative intimacy of the theatre and the artificial lighting. The play poses no major staging challenges and the various effects and properties were well within the normal range of a theatre company of the period. Trained young male actors would have played the female parts.

Although *The Changeling* is now regarded as one of the masterpieces of Jacobean drama, it appears not to have been performed between the end of the seventeenth century and the 1950s. This theatrical eclipse partly stemmed from the play's subject matter, since plays that involved sexual partners being substituted for others were considered too immoral for polite society. Critics such as T. S. Eliot and M. C. Bradbrook paved the way for a critical reassessment of the play that led in due course to a series of revivals since 1950 that have re-established the play in the theatrical canon.

In *The Changeling* the authors created a dramatic structure that gives memorable dynamic form to the moral and psychological issues it raises. In particular they use a number of dramatic, theatrical, thematic and linguistic strategies to bind the actions and the characters of the play together almost subliminally. Although the visual, almost emblematic moments (particularly the dropped handkerchief, the ring and the finger, and the dumbshow) play a major part in this process, the relationship between the plot and the subplot, the concepts associated with changelings and the linked ideas of change and exchange are crucial factors in the play's structure.

A changeling is either a child left by the fairies in exchange for one they take away or the child they take away itself. Characteristically, the child left behind in the mortal world is physically or mentally abnormal. Presumably the idea originated in a desire to explain the otherwise apparently random appearance of such children. Inevitably the term came to be extended to apply to various categories of those with mental or physical disabilities. It is in this sense that it is applicable to Antonio in the subplot, who pretends to be an idiot and is, strictly, the changeling of the title.

Plot and Subplot

Middleton and Rowley wrote *The Changeling* jointly. There is still some critical suspicion of multi-authored works because the post-Romantic critical tradition still values the author's supposed 'individual voice' and 'originality' far more highly than the Jacobean dramatists did as they struggled to earn their livings in a precarious theatrical business. Despite the influential criticism of Roland Barthes and more recent approaches attacking the idea of the authority of the author, there is still a powerful tendency to see collaborative works in terms of who wrote which bits, who was the originator, who gave the instructions. However, it is grossly misleading to see the play as two disparate stories by two authors, linked only in the revelations of the last act. In fact, although there is very little narrative interdependence between the two plots, they are related thematically and structurally in ways that are crucial to the play's overall effectiveness. It is possible to stage the Beatrice-Joanna/De Flores plot without the Isabella story (as the various television versions demonstrate) but what the play may seem to gain as a concentrated study of an isolated individual, it loses by not offering the wider perspectives provided by the values of the world outside Vermandero's household. This other world, the world of the madhouse, provides a corrective commentary on Beatrice-Joanna's behaviour by showing a positive model of how to behave. It is a kind of ironic reversal of the Shakespearian flight from court to a more natural world seen in plays such *As You Like It*.

Beatrice-Joanna's dealings with her various suitors (Alonzo de Piraquo, De Flores, Alsemero) provide the main impetus of the main plot. The subplot is constructed to give an alternative perspective by treating a similar situation in a radically different way. The emphasis is, broadly, comic, since no real harm comes to the characters in the subplot, and the relationship between Alibius and Isabella is re-established on a basis of mutual trust rather than jealousy. The central characters of the subplot are not as important socially as the characters in the main plot but their moral behaviour is better, particularly if we compare Isabella with Beatrice-Joanna.

The subplot is not comic relief but a working out of the moral issues from a different perspective. In the more overt world of the subplot potential lovers adopt physical disguises in their efforts to gain their beloved. Isabella's physical world is dominated by the two wards of madmen and fools: it is a world where those who do not conform to society's codes are incarcerated, yet it is also a world where those codes are more strictly observed than they are in the fashionable world of Beatrice-Joanna. In traditional comic terms, Isabella has every reason to cuckold her husband: he is old, jealous without cause and treats her badly. Yet in the face of the two would-be lovers' advances she remains constant and is eventually rewarded by her husband's confidence in her when she reveals the plot to him. There is a striking theatrical enactment of this in Act 4 Scene 3, when she adopts the physical disguise of a madwoman and Antonio fails to see through it. Isabella can change into a new shape, the outward appearance of a madwoman, but is able to return to her original one, unlike her counterpart, Beatrice-Joanna, who is trapped in a series of metamorphoses and cannot return.

The relationship between the Beatrice-Joanna and Isabella plots is not simply one of parallels, because the range of choices available to each of them differs and their reactions to them are dissimilar. It is also important that although the action of the subplot takes place in a madhouse, the main characters of that plot are sane, merely adopting disguises in order to get closer to Isabella. On the other hand, in the ostensibly sane world of the main plot, the characters behave in ways that can be considered mad. Middleton and Rowley take great care to

provide alternative perspectives on each plot. Thus, Isabella
stays loyal to her husband whereas Beatrice-Joanna aban-
dons her loyalty to her fiancé and her father. De Flores
and Lollio both demand sexual favours for keeping quiet,
but whereas De Flores is successful, Isabella threatens
Lollio with death at Antonio's hands in an ironic counterpart to De Flores' murder of Alonzo. The structure of the
play is important here, since, by placing Lollio's demands
on Isabella after Alonzo's murder but before De Flores
asks for his reward, the authors bring two possible modes
of behaviour in similar situations into a very close
juxtaposition.

Finally the connection between the two plots is made very
explicit at the end of the play when Alsemero sums up the
action of the main plot, beginning with the moon, that
perennial symbol of change:

> What an opaque body had that moon
> That last chang'd on us! Here's beauty chang'd
> To ugly whoredom; here, servant obedience
> To a master sin, imperious murder;
> I, a supposed husband, chang'd embraces
> With wantonness, but that was paid before;
> Your change is come too, from an ignorant wrath
> To knowing friendship. Are there any more on's?
>
> (5.3.197-204)

And the false fool, the false madman, the tempted wife
and the jealous husband all admit their membership of the
club, each, inevitably, using the word change. So, between
the two plots we are presented with an image of a whole
society affected in various ways by the influence of 'love's

tame madness', which is what Tomazo calls Alonzo's love in Act 2 Scene 1 when he sees that Beatrice-Joanna is no longer as affectionate as she was. In some cases, the madness leads to death; in others it comes close, as society changes from an apparently ordered situation to one where its hidden desires and fantasies are given full expression for a while, with catastrophic results.

Changelings, Changes, Exchanges

As the play's title suggests, the ideas of change and exchange associated with changelings provide one of its most important organising principles. The importance of the subplot is most obvious in the fact that the notions associated with changelings are to be found there. Some of the ideas of change and exchange are more significant than others and almost any play will, inevitably, show the characters changing in some ways. In *The Changeling*, however, the changes are actually related causally and thematically so that they are dependent on one another and also related to the theme of the deceptiveness of outward appearance until the situation changes and the concealed truth emerges. The key element in this complex of ideas is that someone is changed or exchanged, and this allows the concept to be applied almost universally throughout the play.

For Antonio and Franciscus the change is simple: by adopting the roles of the fool and the madman, both pretend to be something different from what they actually are. In the case of Alibius the idea works in two ways: his name is formed from *alibi*, the Latin word which means he is somewhere else while something is going on, but he is also changed from being an unjustly jealous husband to one who has confidence in his wife; he will 'change now/into a better'. Just as Franciscus and Antonio adopt disguises, so does Isabella who is not recognised by her putative lover when she disguises herself as a madwoman.

Beatrice-Joanna and De Flores initiate many of the changes that occur to other members of the cast. De Flores is apparently physically ugly – at least Beatrice-Joanna tells us that he is, though no one else seems worried by his appearance – and this physical ugliness could be characteristic of a changeling. He is also the instrument of change since he actually does all the dirty work: he kills Alonzo, the most fundamental change of all, thus allowing Beatrice-Joanna to change from being engaged to him to being engaged to Alsemero. He changes Beatrice-Joanna from a virgin to a whore; he kills Diaphanta after she has exchanged her virginity for experience. He also changes in Beatrice-Joanna's judgment of him, from an ugly to a beloved man and, in other people's judgment, from 'honest' De Flores to 'horrid villain' when the truth is finally revealed.

The changes in Beatrice-Joanna are equally significant and relate not only to the original meaning of 'changeling;' but also to one of its extended connotations, that of 'a woman whose affections were not constant'. After all, she starts the play engaged to Alonzo but changes her affections to Alsemero and ultimately to De Flores. The successive changes chart her decline morally, spiritually and socially. This is particularly evident in the great exchange between her and De Flores in Act 3, Scene 4, where Beatrice-

Joanna tries to evade the consequences of her desires and
De Flores replies:

> Though thou writ'st maid, thou whore in thy affection!
> 'Twas chang'd from thy first love, and that's a kind
> Of whoredom in thy heart; and he's chang'd now,
> To bring thy second on, thy Alsemero,
> Whom (by all the sweets that ever darkness tasted)
> If I enjoy thee not, thou ne'er enjoy'st.   (3.4.143-8)

Beatrice-Joanna is also a changeling in her dissimilarity to
her father. Vermandero is a decent man, a careful father
trying to do his best for his daughter, whereas Beatrice-
Joanna has no compunction about telling lies, organising
murders, and cheating her husband. Finally she says as
much to her father: 'O come not near me, sir, I shall
defile you:/ I am that of your blood was taken from
you/For your better health; look no more upon't, / But
cast it to the ground regardlessly' (5.3.149-52).

Visual Elements

The visual elements of the play have an important
function in presenting the transformations and excesses
associated with the outbreak of changing emotions.

For example, the dropping of Beatrice-Joanna's glove in
the first scene is a highly visual way of showing the
alterations that occur in people's plans. She drops it as a
love token for Alsemero but De Flores picks it up. This
highly conventional lover's gesture is meant as a signal of
Beatrice-Joanna's changed affections but actually operates
as a prophetic anticipation of what is really going to

happen in the play. Beatrice-Joanna's glove dropping is a
visual presentation of her willing change from Alonzo and
her initially unwilling change to De Flores, showing her
impetuousness, since she miscalculates the relative physical
(and mental) positions of her father, De Flores and
Alsemero. She wants to give Alsemero a love token, but
she doesn't see the situation properly.

Beatrice-Joanna's blindness to the possible consequences
of her actions also appears in her reaction to the physical
evidence of Alonzo's death. When De Flores presents her
with Alonzo's finger it gives her a sense of the reality of
what she has become involved in and it colours our
attitude to her during the crucial scene with De Flores
after the murder (3.4). The fact that the ring would not
come off the finger is important symbolically: the ring was
given to Alonzo by Beatrice-Joanna as a love token, De
Flores brings it back, like a cat bringing a present to its
owner, as a token of <u>his</u> love. She tells him to keep it,
thus symbolically giving it and herself to him. The ring is
one of many sexual symbols in the play and its symbolism
is partly carried over from the business with the glove
where De Flores talked about thrusting his fingers into
Beatrice-Joanna's sockets. In both incidents the visual is
reinforced verbally, but a considerable amount of meaning
is derived from the physical action.

The Changeling in the Modern World

In many ways the Beatrice-Joanna story is a domestic
tragedy. Although it is set in the citadel at Alicante, there
are no important political issues at stake, no empires

crumble, no states totter. A verse form that is very flexible and colloquial, bound together by repeated use of words, matches the inherently domestic setting. However, the authors also use image clusters such as allusions to the Fall of Man, concepts of change and perception, allusions to hell, and words like 'blood', 'will', 'act', 'service' and 'deed' (which are particularly associated with De Flores, usually in a sexual context) to link the characters, indicating, almost subliminally, that they are trapped in the same linguistic and dramatic framework. However domestic and colloquial the play may be, it is not naturalistic in approach: the dumb show, the virginity test and the substitute bed-mate trick are all powerful reminders of the play's theatrical and intellectual contexts.

In his essay on Middleton, T. S. Eliot suggested that *The Changeling* is 'the tragedy of the not naturally bad but irresponsible nature caught in the consequences of its own action'. He was referring to Beatrice-Joanna and her relationship with De Flores, though his comment could apply equally well to the two noblemen who disguise themselves for the love of Isabella and nearly get executed because of their apparent guilt for Alonzo's death. Eliot's remark goes close to the heart of the whole play, to its presentation of people who don't stop to think, whose moral vision is limited, who see only the desired object at the end of their actions and ignore possible ramifications and potential consequences. Beatrice-Joanna is clearly the classic example here, as her desire to marry one man rather than another leads to catastrophe after catastrophe. A major part of the impact of the tragedy and a significant factor in its modern appeal, lies precisely in the

way that the authors show us characters who are unable
to see that the methods they adopt to achieve ends which
may, in themselves, be honourable and legitimate
disqualify them from successfully achieving the desired
result. The compelling horror of the play lies in its
convincing presentation of just how easy it is to step over
the line that divides proper from improper behaviour,
from the banal to the tragic, and just how destructive the
unrestrained acting out of subconscious desires can be.

Trevor R Griffiths

The text of this edition is based on the 1653 quarto, with
lightly modernised spelling and punctuation. Square
brackets indicate words added to the quarto text.

Middleton and Rowley: Key Dates

Further Reading

The Changeling is discussed in classic studies such as
M.C. Bradbrook's *Themes and Conventions of Elizabethan
Tragedy* (1935), Una Ellis-Fermor's *The Jacobean Drama*
(1936) and Irving Ribner's *Jacobean Drama* (1962).
T.S. Eliot's 1927 essay on Middleton is reprinted in his
Elizabethan Dramatists (1963) and elsewhere. *The Cambridge
Companion to English Renaissance Drama* (eds. A.R. Braunmuller
and Michael Hattaway, 1990) provides authoritative
accounts of the social and theatrical contexts and guides
to further reading. Alexander Leggatt's *English Drama:
Shakespeare to the Restoration* (1988) is a useful survey of
Renaissance drama. Michael Scott discusses modern
revivals in *Renaissance Drama and a Modern Audience* (1982).
Staging the Renaissance (1991), edited by David Scott Kastan
and Peter Stallybrass, reprints some significant modern
essays on many aspects of Renaissance theatre.

THE CHANGELING

Dramatis Personae

VERMANDERO, *father to Beatrice*
TOMAZO DE PIRACQUO, *a noble lord*
ALONZO DE PIRACQUO, *his brother, suitor to Beatrice*
ALSEMERO, *a nobleman, afterwards married to Beatrice*
JASPERINO, *his friend*
ALIBIUS, *a jealous doctor*
LOLLIO, *his man*
PEDRO, *friend to Antonio*
ANTONIO, *the changeling*
FRANCISCUS, *the counterfeit madman*
DE FLORES, *servant to Vermandero*
Madmen [and Fools]
[Gentlemen and Gallants]
Servants

BEATRICE [JOANNA], *daughter to Vermandero*
DIAPHANTA, *her waiting-woman*
ISABELLA, *wife to Alibius*
[Gentlewomen]

The Scene: Alligant [i.e., Alicante].

ACT ONE

[Scene i]

Enter ALSEMERO.

ALSEMERO. 'Twas in the temple where I first beheld her,
   And now again the same; what omen yet
   Follows of that? None but imaginary;
   Why should my hopes or fate be timorous?
   The place is holy, so is my intent:
   I love her beauties to the holy purpose,
   And that, methinks, admits comparison
   With man's first creation, the place blest,
   And is his right home back, if he achieve it.
   The church hath first begun our interview   10
   And that's the place must join us into one,
   So there's beginning and perfection too.

Enter JASPERINO.

JASPERINO. O sir, are you here? Come, the wind's fair
    with you,
   Y'are like to have a swift and pleasant passage.

ALSEMERO. Sure y'are deceived, friend, 'tis contrary
   In my best judgment.

JASPERINO.   What, for Malta?
   If you could buy a gale amongst the witches,
   They could not serve you such a lucky pennyworth
   As comes a' God's name.

ALSEMERO.   Even now I observ'd
  The temple's vane to turn full in my face,   20
  I know 'tis against me.

JASPERINO.   Against you?
  Then you know not where you are.

ALSEMERO.   Not well indeed.

JASPERINO. Are you not well, sir?

ALSEMERO.   Yes, Jasperino.
  Unless there be some hidden malady
  Within me, that I understand not.

JASPERINO.   And that
  I begin to doubt, sir; I never knew
  Your inclinations to travels at a pause
  With any cause to hinder it till now.
  Ashore you were wont to call your servants up,
  And help to trap your horses for the speed.   30
  At sea I have seen you weigh the anchor with 'em,
  Hoist sails for fear to lose the foremost breath,
  Be in continual prayers for fair winds,
  And have you chang'd your orisons?

ALSEMERO.   No, friend,
  I keep the same church, same devotion.

JASPERINO. Lover I'm sure y'are none, the stoic
  Was found in you long ago; your mother
  Nor best friends, who have set snares of beauty,
  Ay, and choice ones too, could never trap you that way.
  What might be the cause?

ALSEMERO.   Lord, how violent   40
  Thou art; I was but meditating of
  Somewhat I heard within the temple.

JASPERINO. Is this violence? 'Tis but idleness
　　Compar'd with your haste yesterday.

ALSEMERO. I'm all this while a-going, man.

　　Enter SERVANTS.

JASPERINO. Backwards, I think, sir. Look, your servants.

SERVANT 1. The seamen call; shall we board your trunks?

ALSEMERO. No, not today.

JASPERINO. 'Tis the critical day, it seems, and the sign in
　　Aquarius.

SERVANT 2 [*aside*]. We must not to sea today; this　　　　50
　　smoke will bring forth fire.

ALSEMERO. Keep all on shore; I do not know the end
　　(Which needs I must do) of an affair in hand
　　Ere I can go to sea.

SERVANT 1. Well, your pleasure.

SERVANT 2 [*aside*]. Let him e'en take his leisure too, we are
　　safer on land.

　　Exeunt SERVANTS. *Enter* BEATRICE, DIAPHANTA, *and*
　　SERVANTS. [ALSEMERO *greets* BEATRICE *and kisses her.*]

JASPERINO [*aside*]. How now! The laws of the Medes are
　　chang'd sure! Salute a woman? He kisses too: wonderful!
　　Where learnt he this? And does it perfectly too; in　　　60
　　my conscience he ne'er rehears'd it before. Nay, go
　　on, this will be stranger and better news at Valencia
　　than if he had ransom'd half Greece from the Turk.

BEATRICE. You are a scholar, sir?

ALSEMERO.　　　　　　　　A weak one, lady.

BEATRICE. Which of the sciences is this love you speak of?

ALSEMERO. From your tongue I take it to be music.

BEATRICE. You are skilful in't, can sing at first sight.

ALSEMERO. And I have show'd you all my skill at once.
    I want more words to express me further
    And must be forc'd to repetition: 70
    I love you dearly.

BEATRICE.   Be better advis'd, sir:
    Our eyes are sentinels unto our judgments,
    And should give certain judgment what they see;
    But they are rash sometimes, and tell us wonders
    Of common things, which when our judgments find,
    They can then check the eyes, and call them blind.

ALSEMERO. But I am further, lady; yesterday
    Was mine eyes' employment, and hither now
    They brought my judgment, where are both agreed.
    Both Houses then consenting, 'tis agreed,   80
    Only there wants the confirmation
    By the hand royal, that's your part, lady.

BEATRICE. O there's one above me, sir. [*Aside.*] For five
        days past
    To be recall'd! Sure, mine eyes were mistaken,
    This was the man was meant me; that he should come
    So near his time, and miss it!

JASPERINO [*aside*]. We might have come by the carriers
    from Valencia, I see, and sav'd all our sea-provision: we
    are at farthest sure. Methinks I should do something
    too; I mean to be a venturer in this voyage. Yonder's   90
    another vessel, I'll board her; if she be lawful prize,
    down goes her topsail.

[Approaches DIAPHANTA.] *Enter* DE FLORES.

DE FLORES. Lady, your father –

BEATRICE.   Is in health, I hope.

DE FLORES. Your eye shall instantly instruct you, lady.
  He's coming hitherward.

BEATRICE.   What needed then
  Your duteous preface? I had rather
  He had come unexpected; you must stall
  A good presence with unnecessary blabbing:
  And how welcome for your part you are,
  I'm sure you know.

DE FLORES *[aside].* Will't never mend this scorn   100
  One side nor other? Must I be enjoin'd
  To follow still whilst she flies from me? Well,
  Fates do your worst, I'll please myself with sight
  Of her, at all opportunities,
  If but to spite her anger; I know she had
  Rather see me dead than living, and yet
  She knows no cause for't, but a peevish will.

ALSEMERO. You seem'd displeas'd, lady, on the sudden.

BEATRICE. Your pardon, sir, 'tis my infirmity,
  Nor can I other reason render you,   110
  Than his or hers, of some particular thing
  They must abandon as a deadly poison,
  Which to a thousand other tastes were wholesome;
  Such to mine eyes is that same fellow there,
  The same that report speaks of the basilisk.

ALSEMERO. This is a frequent frailty in our nature;
  There's scarce a man amongst a thousand sound
  But hath his imperfection: one distastes

The scent of roses, which to infinites
Most pleasing is, and odoriferous;   120
One oil, the enemy of poison;
Another wine, the cheerer of the heart,
And lively refresher of the countenance.
Indeed this fault (if so it be) is general,
There's scarce a thing but is both lov'd and loath'd.
Myself (I must confess) have the same frailty.

BEATRICE. And what may be your poison, sir? I am
    bold with you.

ALSEMERO. What might be your desire, perhaps, a cherry.

BEATRICE. I am no enemy to any creature
My memory has, but yon gentleman.   130

ALSEMERO. He does ill to tempt your sight, if he knew it.

BEATRICE. He cannot be ignorant of that, sir,
I have not spar'd to tell him so; and I want
To help myself, since he's a gentleman
In good respect with my father, and follows him.

ALSEMERO. He's out of his place then now.

[*They talk apart.*]

JASPERINO. I am a mad wag, wench.

DIAPHANTA. So methinks; but for your comfort I can
    tell you, we have a doctor in the city that undertakes
    the cure of such.   140

JASPERINO. Tush, I know what physic is best for the state
    of mine own body.

DIAPHANTA. 'Tis scarce a well-govern'd state, I believe.

JASPERINO. I could show thee such a thing with an

ingredient that we two would compound together, and
if it did not tame the maddest blood i' th'town for two
hours after, I'll ne'er profess physic again.

DIAPHANTA. A little poppy, sir, were good to cause
you sleep.

JASPERINO. Poppy? I'll give thee a pop i'th'lips for   150
that first, and begin there. [*Kisses her.*] Poppy is
one simple indeed, and cuckoo (what you call't)
another: I'll discover no more now, another time
I'll show thee all.

BEATRICE. My father, sir.

Enter VERMANDERO *and* SERVANTS.

VERMANDERO. O Joanna, I came to meet thee;
Your devotion's ended?

BEATRICE.   For this time, sir.
[*Aside.*] I shall change my saint, I fear me, I find
A giddy turning in me; Sir, this while
I am beholding to this gentleman   160
Who left his own way to keep me company,
And in discourse I find him much desirous
To see your castle: he hath deserv'd it, sir,
If ye please to grant it.

VERMANDERO.   With all my heart, sir.
Yet there's an article between, I must know
Your country; we use not to give survey
Of our chief strengths to strangers; our citadels
Are plac'd conspicuous to outward view
On promonts' tops; but within are secrets.

ALSEMERO. A Valencian, sir.   170

VERMANDERO.   A Valencian?

That's native, sir; of what name, I beseech you?

ALSEMERO. Alsemero, sir.

VERMANDERO.   Alsemero; not the son
  Of John de Alsemero?

ALSEMERO.   The same, sir.

VERMANDERO. My best love bids you welcome.

BEATRICE [*aside*].   He was wont
  To call me so, and then he speaks a most
  Unfeigned truth.

VERMANDERO.   O sir, I knew your father.
  We two were in acquaintance long ago,
  Before our chins were worth Iulan down,
  And so continued till the stamp of time   180
  Had coin'd us into silver: well, he's gone;
  A good soldier went with him.

ALSEMERO. You went together in that, sir.

VERMANDERO. No, by Saint Jacques, I came behind him.
  Yet I have done somewhat too; an unhappy day
  Swallowed him at last at Gibraltar
  In fight with those rebellious Hollanders,
  Was it not so?

ALSEMERO.   Whose death I had reveng'd
  Or followed him in fate, had not the late league
  Prevented me.

VERMANDERO. Ay, ay, 'twas time to breathe: 190
  O Joanna, I should ha' told thee news,
  I saw Piracquo lately.

BEATRICE [*aside*].   That's ill news.

VERMANDERO. He's hot preparing for his day of triumph,
    Thou must be a bride within this sevennight.

ALSEMERO [*aside*].   Ha!

BEATRICE. Nay, good sir, be not so violent; with speed
    I cannot render satisfaction
    Unto the dear companion of my soul,
    Virginity, whom I thus long have liv'd with,
    And part with it so rude and suddenly;
    Can such friends divide, never to meet again,   200
    Without a solemn farewell?

VERMANDERO.   Tush, tush, there's a toy.

ALSEMERO [*aside*]. I must now part, and never meet again
    With any joy on earth; Sir, your pardon,
    My affairs call on me.

VERMANDERO.   How, sir? By no means;
    Not chang'd so soon, I hope? You must see my castle
    And her best entertainment ere we part;
    I shall think myself unkindly us'd else.
    Come, come, let's on; I had good hope your stay
    Had been a while with us in Alligant;
    I might have bid you to my daughter's wedding.   210

ALSEMERO [*aside*]. He means to feast me, and poisons
    me beforehand.
    I should be dearly glad to be there, sir,
    Did my occasions suit as I could wish.

BEATRICE. I shall be sorry if you be not there
    When it is done, sir, but not so suddenly.

VERMANDERO. I tell you, sir, the gentleman's complete,
    A courtier and a gallant, enrich'd
    With many fair and noble ornaments.
    I would not change him for a son-in-law

For any he in Spain, the proudest he,   220
And we have great ones, that you know.

ALSEMERO.   He's much
Bound to you, sir.

VERMANDERO.   He shall be bound to me,
As fast as this tie can hold him; I'll want my will else.

BEATRICE [*aside*]. I shall want mine if you do it.

VERMANDERO. But come, by the way I'll tell you more
of him.

VERMANDERO [*aside*]. How shall I dare to venture in
his castle,
When he discharges murderers at the gate?
But I must on, for back I cannot go.

BEATRICE [*aside*]. Not this serpent gone yet?

[*Drops her glove.*]

VERMANDERO.   Look, girl, thy glove's fall'n;
Stay, stay. – De Flores, help a little.

[*Exeunt* VERMANDERO, ALSEMERO, JASPERINO, *and*
SERVANTS.]

DE FLORES [*offering glove*].   Here, lady.   230

BEATRICE. Mischief on your officious forwardness!
Who bade you stoop? They touch my hand no more:
There, for tother's sake I part with this,

[*Takes off the other glove and throws it down.*]

Take 'em and draw thine own skin off with 'em.

Exeunt [*all but* DE FLORES].

DE FLORES. Here's a favour come, with a mischief! Now

I know
She had rather wear my pelt tann'd in a pair
Of dancing pumps, than I should thrust my fingers
Into her sockets here. I know she hates me,
Yet cannot choose but love her:
No matter, if but to vex her, I'll haunt her still;   240
Though I get nothing else, I'll have my will.

Exit.

[Scene ii]

Enter ALIBIUS *and* LOLLIO.

ALIBIUS. Lollio, I must trust thee with a secret,
But thou must keep it.

LOLLIO. I was ever close to a secret, sir.

ALIBIUS. The diligence that I have found in thee,
The care and industry already past,
Assures me of thy good continuance.
Lollio, I have a wife.

LOLLIO. Fie sir, 'tis too late to keep her secret, she's known to
be married all the town and country over.

ALIBIUS. Thou goest too fast, my Lollio; that knowledge   10
I allow no man can be barr'd it;
But there is a knowledge which is nearer,
Deeper and sweeter, Lollio.

LOLLIO. Well, sir, let us handle that between you and I.

ALIBIUS. 'Tis that I go about, man; Lollio,
My wife is young.

LOLLIO. So much the worse to be kept secret, sir.

ALIBIUS. Why, now thou meet'st the substance of the point;
I am old, Lollio.

LOLLIO. No, sir, 'tis I am old Lollio.   20

ALIBIUS. Yet why may not this concord and sympathize?
Old trees and young plants often grow together,
Well enough agreeing.

LOLLIO. Ay, sir, but the old trees raise themselves higher
and broader than the young plants.

ALIBIUS. Shrewd application! There's the fear, man;
I would wear my ring on my own finger;
Whilst it is borrowed it is none of mine,
But his that useth it.

LOLLIO. You must keep it on still then; if it but lie by,   30
one or other will be thrusting into't.

ALIBIUS. Thou conceiv'st me, Lollio; here thy watchful eye
Must have employment, I cannot always be at home.

LOLLIO. I dare swear you cannot.

ALIBIUS. I must look out.

LOLLIO. I know't, you must look out, 'tis every man's case.

ALIBIUS. Here I do say must thy employment be:
To watch her treadings, and in my absence
Supply my place.

LOLLIO. I'll do my best, sir, yet surely I cannot see   40
who you should have cause to be jealous of.

ALIBIUS. Thy reason for that, Lollio? 'Tis a comfortable
question.

LOLLIO. We have but two sorts of people in the house, and
both under the whip, that's fools and madmen; the one has
not wit enough to be knaves, and the other not knavery
enough to be fools.

ALIBIUS. Ay, those are all my patients, Lollio.
I do profess the cure of either sort:
My trade, my living 'tis, I thrive by it;   50
But here's the care that mixes with my thrift:
The daily visitants, that come to see
My brainsick patients, I would not have
To see my wife: gallants I do observe
Of quick enticing eyes, rich in habits,
Of stature and proportion very comely:
These are most shrewd temptations, Lollio.

LOLLIO. They may be easily answered, sir; if they come to
see the fools and madmen, you and I may serve the turn,
and let my mistress alone, she's of neither sort.   60

ALIBIUS. 'Tis a good ward; indeed, come they to see
Our madmen or our fools, let 'em see no more
Than what they come for; by that consequent
They must not see her, I'm sure she's no fool.

LOLLIO. And I'm sure she's no madman.

ALIBIUS. Hold that buckler fast, Lollio; my trust
Is on thee, and I account it firm and strong.
What hour is't, Lollio?

LOLLIO. Towards belly-hour, sir.

ALIBIUS. Dinner time? Thou mean'st twelve o'clock.   70

LOLLIO. Yes, sir, for every part has his hour: we wake at six
and look about us, that's eye-hour; at seven we should pray,
that's knee-hour; at eight walk, that's leg-hour; at nine gather

flowers and pluck a rose, that's nose-hour; at ten we drink,
that's mouth-hour; at eleven lay about us for victuals, that's
hand-hour; at twelve go to dinner, that's belly-hour.

ALIBIUS. Profoundly, Lollio! It will be long
Ere all thy scholars learn this lesson, and
I did look to have a new one entered – Stay,   80
I think my expectation is come home.

Enter PEDRO, *and* ANTONIO *like an idiot.*

PEDRO. Save you, sir; my business speaks itself,
This sight takes off the labour of my tongue.

ALIBIUS. Ay, ay, sir,
'Tis plain enough, you mean him for my patient.

PEDRO. And if your pains prove but commodious, to give but
some little strength to his sick and weak part of nature in
him, these [*Gives money.*] are but patterns to show you of the
whole pieces that will follow to you, beside the charge of
diet, washing, and other necessaries fully defrayed.   91

ALIBIUS. Believe it, sir, there shall no care be wanting.

LOLLIO. Sir, an officer in this place may deserve something;
the trouble will pass through my hands.

PEDRO. 'Tis fit something should come to your hands then,
sir.

[*Gives money.*]

LOLLIO. Yes, sir, 'tis I must keep him sweet, and read to him;
what is his name?

PEDRO. His name is Antonio; marry, we use but half to him,
only Tony.

LOLLIO. Tony, Tony, 'tis enough, and a very good name for a

    fool; what's your name, Tony?   101

ANTONIO. He, he, he! Well, I thank you, cousin, he, he, he!

LOLLIO. Good boy! Hold up your head: he can laugh,
    I perceive by that he is no beast.

PEDRO. Well, sir,
    If you can raise him but to any height,
    Any degree of wit, might he attain
    (As I might say) to creep but on all four
    Towards the chair of wit, or walk on crutches,
    'Twould add an honour to your worthy pains,   110
    And a great family might pray for you,
    To which he should be heir, had he discretion
    To claim and guide his own; assure you, sir,
    He is a gentleman.

LOLLIO. Nay, there's nobody doubted that; at first sight
    I knew him for a gentleman, he looks no other yet.

PEDRO. Let him have good attendance and sweet lodging.

LOLLIO. As good as my mistress lies in, sir; and as you allow
    us time and means, we can raise him to the higher degree of
    discretion.   120

PEDRO. Nay, there shall no cost want, sir.

LOLLIO. He will hardly be stretch'd up to the wit of a
    magnifico.

PEDRO. O no, that's not to be expected, far shorter will be
    enough.

LOLLIO. I'll warrant you [I'll] make him fit to bear office in
    five weeks; I'll undertake to wind him up to the wit of
    constable.

PEDRO. If it be lower than that it might serve turn.   129

LOLLIO. No, fie, to level him with a headborough, beadle, or watchman were but little better than he is; constable I'll able him: if he do come to be a Justice afterwards, let him thank the keeper. Or I'll go further with you; say I do bring him up to my own pitch, say I make him as wise as myself.

PEDRO. Why, there I would have it.

LOLLIO. Well, go to, either I'll be as errant a fool as he, or he shall be as wise as I, and then I think 'twill serve his turn.

PEDRO. Nay, I do like thy wit passing well.   140

LOLLIO. Yes, you may; yet if I had not been a fool, I had had more wit than I have too; remember what state you find me in.

PEDRO. I will, and so leave you: your best cares, I beseech you.

ALIBIUS. Take you none with you, leave 'em all with us.

Exit PEDRO.

ANTONIO. O my cousin's gone! Cousin, cousin! O!

LOLLIO. Peace, peace Tony, you must not cry, child, you must be whipp'd if you do; your cousin is here still, I am your cousin, Tony.   150

ANTONIO. He, he! Then I'll not cry, if thou be'st my cousin, he, he, he!

LOLLIO. I were best try his wit a little, that I may know what form to place him in.

ALIBIUS. Ay, do, Lollio, do.

LOLLIO. I must ask him easy questions at first: Tony, how
    many true fingers has a tailor on his right hand?

ANTONIO. As many as on his left, cousin.

LOLLIO. Good; and how many on both?

ANTONIO. Two less than a deuce, cousin.   160

LOLLIO. Very well answered; I come to you again, cousin
    Tony: how many fools goes to a wise man?

ANTONIO. Forty in a day sometimes, cousin.

LOLLIO. Forty in a day? How prove you that?

ANTONIO. All that fall out amongst themselves, and go to a
    lawyer to be made friends.

LOLLIO. A parlous fool! He must sit in the fourth form at
    least, I perceive that; I come again, Tony: how many knaves
    make an honest man?

ANTONIO. I know not that, cousin.   170

LOLLIO. No, the question is too hard for you: I'll tell you,
    cousin, there's three knaves may make an honest man, a
    sergeant, a jailer, and a beadle; the sergeant catches him, the
    jailer holds him, and the beadle lashes him; and if he be not
    honest then, the hangman must cure him.

ANTONIO. Ha, ha, ha, that's fine sport, cousin!

ALIBIUS. This was too deep a question for the fool, Lollio.

LOLLIO. Yes, this might have serv'd yourself, though I say't;
    once more, and you shall go play, Tony.

ANTONIO. Ay, play at push-pin, cousin, ha, he!   180

LOLLIO. So thou shalt; say how many fools are here.

ANTONIO. Two, cousin, thou and I.

LOLLIO. Nay, y'are too forward there, Tony; mark my
  question: how many fools and knaves are here? A fool
  before a knave, a fool behind a knave, between every two
  fools a knave; how many fools, how many knaves?

ANTONIO. I never learnt so far, cousin.

ALIBIUS. Thou put'st too hard questions to him, Lollio.

LOLLIO. I'll make him understand it easily; cousin, stand
  there.   190

ANTONIO. Ay, cousin.

LOLLIO. Master, stand you next the fool.

ALIBIUS. Well, Lollio?

LOLLIO. Here's my place: mark now, Tony, there a fool
  before a knave.

ANTONIO. That's I, cousin.

LOLLIO. Here's a fool behind a knave, that's I, and between
  us two fools there is a knave, that's my master; 'tis but we
  three, that's all.

ANTONIO. We three, we three, cousin!   200

  MADMEN *within*.

MADMAN 1. Put's head i'th'pillory, the bread's too little.

MADMAN 2. Fly, fly, and he catches the swallow.

MADMAN 3. Give her more onion, or the Devil put the rope
  about her crag.

LOLLIO. You may hear what time of day it is, the chimes of
  Bedlam goes.

ALIBIUS. Peace, peace, or the wire comes!

MADMAN 3. Cat whore, cat whore, her permasant, her
     permasant!

ALIBIUS. Peace, I say; their hour's come, they must be   210
     fed, Lollio.

LOLLIO. There's no hope of recovery of that Welsh madman,
     was undone by a mouse, that spoil'd him a permasant; lost
     his wits for't.

ALIBIUS. Go to your charge, Lollio, I'll to mine.

LOLLIO. Go you to your madmen's ward, let me alone with
     your fools.

ALIBIUS. And remember my last charge, Lollio.

Exit.

LOLLIO. Of which your patients do you think I am?
     Come, Tony, you must amongst your school-fellows   220
     now; there's pretty scholars amongst 'em, I can tell
     you, there's some of 'em at *stultus, stulta, stultum.*

ANTONIO. I would see the madmen, cousin, if they would
     not bite me.

LOLLIO. No, they shall not bite thee, Tony.

ANTONIO. They bite when they are at dinner, do they not,
     cuz?

LOLLIO. They bite at dinner indeed, Tony. Well, I
     hope to get credit by thee, I like thee the best of
     all the scholars that ever I brought up, and thou   230
     shalt prove a wise man, or I'll prove a fool myself.

Exeunt.

ACT TWO

[Scene i]

Enter BEATRICE *and* JASPERINO *severally.*

BEATRICE. O sir, I'm ready now for that fair service,
    Which makes the name of friend sit glorious on you.
    Good angels and this conduct be your guide,

[*Gives a paper.*]

    Fitness of time and place is there set down, sir.

JASPERINO. The joy I shall return rewards my service.

Exit.

BEATRICE. How wise is Alsemero in his friend!
    It is a sign he makes his choice with judgment.
    Then I appear in nothing more approv'd
    Than making choice of him;
    For 'tis a principle, he that can choose   10
    That bosom well, who of his thoughts partakes,
    Proves most discreet in every choice he makes.
    Methinks I love now with the eyes of judgment
    And see the way to merit, clearly see it.
    A true deserver like a diamond sparkles,
    In darkness you may see him, that's in absence,
    Which is the greatest darkness falls on love;
    Yet is he best discern'd then
    With intellectual eyesight; what's Piracquo
    My father spends his breath for? And his blessing   20

Is only mine, as I regard his name,
Else it goes from me, and turns head against me,
Transform'd into a curse; some speedy way
Must be rememb'red; he's so forward too,
So urgent that way, scarce allows me breath
To speak to my new comforts.

Enter DE FLORES.

DE FLORES [*aside*].   Yonder's she.
  Whatever ails me? Now a-late especially,
  I can as well be hang'd as refrain seeing her;
  Some twenty times a day, nay, not so little,
  Do I force errands, frame ways and excuses   30
  To come into her sight, and I have small reason for't,
  And less encouragement; for she baits me still
  Every time worse than other, does profess herself
  The cruellest enemy to my face in town,
  At no hand can abide the sight of me,
  As if danger or ill luck hung in my looks.
  I must confess my face is bad enough,
  But I know far worse has better fortune,
  And not endur'd alone, but doted on;
  And yet such pick-hair'd faces, chins like witches', 40
  Here and there five hairs, whispering in a corner,
  As if they grew in fear one of another,
  Wrinkles like troughs, where swine-deformity swills
  The tears of perjury that lie there like wash
  Fallen from the slimy and dishonest eye;
  Yet such a one plucks sweets without restraint
  And has the grace of beauty to his sweet.
  Though my hard fate has thrust me out to servitude,
  I tumbled into th'world a gentleman.
  She turns her blessed eye upon me now   50
  And I'll endure all storms before I part with't.

BEATRICE [*aside*]. Again!
  This ominous ill-fac'd fellow more disturbs me
  Than all my other passions.

DE FLORES [*aside*].   Now't begins again;
  I'll stand this storm of hail though the stones pelt me.

BEATRICE. Thy business? What's thy business?

DE FLORES [*aside*].   Soft and fair,
  I cannot part so soon now.

BEATRICE [*aside*].   The villain's fix'd. –
  Thou standing toad-pool!

DE FLORES [*aside*].   The shower falls amain now.

BEATRICE. Who sent thee? What's thy errand? Leave
    my sight.

DE FLORES. My lord your father charg'd me to deliver   60
  A message to you.

BEATRICE.   What, another since?
  Do't and be hang'd then, let me be rid of thee.

DE FLORES. True service merits mercy.

BEATRICE.   What's thy message?

DE FLORES. Let beauty settle but in patience,
  You shall hear all.

BEATRICE.   A dallying, trifling torment!

DE FLORES. Signor Alonzo de Piracquo, lady,
  Sole brother to Tomazo de Piracquo –

BEATRICE. Slave, when wilt make an end?

DE FLORES [*aside*].   Too soon I shall.

BEATRICE. What all this while of him?

DE FLORES.   The said Alonzo,
    With the foresaid Tomazo –

BEATRICE.   Yet again?   70

DE FLORES. Is new alighted.

BEATRICE [*aside*]:   Vengeance strike the news!
    Thou thing most loath'd, what cause was there in this
    To bring thee to my sight?

DE FLORES.   My lord your father
    Charg'd me to seek you out.

BEATRICE.   Is there no other
    To send his errand by?

DE FLORES.   It seems 'tis my luck
    To be i'th'way still.

BEATRICE.   Get thee from me.

DE FLORES [*aside*].   So,
    Why, am not I an ass to devise ways
    Thus to be rail'd at? I must see her still!
    I shall have a mad qualm within this hour again,
    I know't, and like a common Garden-bull   80
    I do but take breath to be lugg'd again.
    What this may bode I know not; I'll despair the less
    Because there's daily precedents of bad faces
    Belov'd beyond all reason; these foul chops
    May come into favour one day 'mongst his fellows:
    Wrangling has prov'd the mistress of good pastime;
    As children cry themselves asleep, I ha' seen
    Women have chid themselves abed to men.

Exit DE FLORES.

BEATRICE. I never see this fellow, but I think   89
  Of some harm towards me, danger's in my mind still,
  I scarce leave trembling of an hour after.
  The next good mood I find my father in,
  I'll get him quite discarded. O I was
  Lost in this small disturbance and forgot
  Affliction's fiercer torrent that now comes
  To bear down all my comforts.

Enter VERMANDERO, ALONZO, TOMAZO.

VERMANDERO.   Y'are both welcome,
  But an especial one belongs to you, sir,
  To whose most noble name our love presents
  The addition of a son, our son Alonzo.

ALONZO. The treasury of honour cannot bring forth   100
  A title I should more rejoice in, sir.

VERMANDERO. You have improv'd it well; daughter,
    prepare,
  The day will steal upon thee suddenly.

BEATRICE [*aside*]. Howe'er, I will be sure to keep the night,
  If it should come so near me.

[BEATRICE *and* VERMANDERO *talk apart.*]

TOMAZO.   Alonzo.

ALONZO.   Brother?

TOMAZO. In troth I see small welcome in her eye.

ALONZO. Fie, you are too severe a censurer
  Of love in all points, there's no bringing on you;
  If lovers should mark everything a fault,
  Affection would be like an ill-set book,   110
  Whose faults might prove as big as half the volume.

BEATRICE. That's all I do entreat.

VERMANDERO.   It is but reasonable;
  I'll see what my son says to't: son Alonzo,
  Here's a motion made but to reprieve
  A maidenhead three days longer; the request
  Is not far out of reason, for indeed
  The former time is pinching.

ALONZO.   Though my joys
  Be set back so much time as I could wish
  They had been forward, yet since she desires it,
  The time is set as pleasing as before,   120
  I find no gladness wanting.

VERMANDERO. May I ever meet it in that point still:
  Y'are nobly welcome, sirs.

  Exeunt VERMANDERO *and* BEATRICE.

TOMAZO. So did you mark the dullness of her parting now?

ALONZO. What dullness? Thou art so exceptious still!

TOMAZO. Why, let it go then, I am but a fool
  To mark your harms so heedfully.

ALONZO.   Where's the oversight?

TOMAZO. Come, your faith's cozened in her, strongly
      cozened;
  Unsettle your affection with all speed
  Wisdom can bring it to, your peace is ruin'd else.   130
  Think what a torment 'tis to marry one
  Whose heart is leap'd into another's bosom:
  If ever pleasure she receive from thee,
  It comes not in thy name, or of thy gift;
  She lies but with another in thine arms,
  He the half-father unto all thy children

In the conception; if he get 'em not,
She helps to get 'em for him, in his passions;
And how dangerous
And shameful her restraint may go in time to,   140
It is not to be thought on without sufferings.

ALONZO. You speak as if she lov'd some other, then.

TOMAZO. Do you apprehend so slowly?

ALONZO.   Nay, and that
Be your fear only, I am safe enough.
Preserve your friendship and your counsel, brother,
For times of more distress; I should depart
An enemy, a dangerous, deadly one
To any but thyself, that should but think
She knew the meaning of inconstancy,
Much less the use and practice; yet w'are friends.   150
Pray let no more be urg'd; I can endure
Much, till I meet an injury to her,
Then I am not myself. Farewell, sweet brother,
How much w'are bound to heaven to depart lovingly.

Exit.

TOMAZO. Why, here is love's tame madness; thus a man
Quickly steals into his vexation.

Exit.

[Scene ii]

Enter DIAPHANTA *and* ALSEMERO.

DIAPHANTA. The place is my charge, you have kept

    your hour,
And the reward of a just meeting bless you.
I hear my lady coming; complete gentleman,
I dare not be too busy with my praises,
Th'are dangerous things to deal with.

Exit.

ALSEMERO.   This goes well;
These women are the ladies' cabinets,
Things of most precious trust are lock'd into 'em.

Enter BEATRICE.

BEATRICE. I have within mine eye all my desires;
Requests that holy prayers ascend heaven for,
And brings 'em down to furnish our defects,   10
Come not more sweet to our necessities
Than thou unto my wishes.

ALSEMERO.   W'are so like
In our expressions, lady, that unless I borrow
The same words, I shall never find their equals.

[*They embrace.*]

BEATRICE. How happy were this meeting, this embrace,
If it were free from envy! This poor kiss,
It has an enemy, a hateful one,
That wishes poison to't: how well were I now
If there were none such name known as Piracquo,
Nor no such tie as the command of parents,   20
I should be but too much blessed.

ALSEMERO.   One good service
Would strike off both your fears, and I'll go near it too,
Since you are so distress'd; remove the cause,
The command ceases, so there's two fears blown out

With one and the same blast.

BEATRICE.   Pray let me find you, sir.
What might that service be so strangely happy?

ALSEMERO. The honourablest piece 'bout man, valour.
I'll send a challenge to Piracquo instantly.

BEATRICE. How? Call you that extinguishing of fear,
When 'tis the only way to keep it flaming?   30
Are not you ventured in the action,
That's all my joys and comforts? Pray, no more, sir.
Say you prevail'd, you're danger's and not mine then.
The law would claim you from me, or obscurity
Be made the grave to bury you alive.
I'm glad these thoughts come forth; O keep not one
Of this condition, sir; here was a course
Found to bring sorrow on her way to death:
The tears would ne'er 'a' dried, till dust had chok'd 'em.
Blood-guiltiness becomes a fouler visage.   40
[*Aside.*] And now I think on one – I was to blame,
I ha' marr'd so good a market with my scorn;
'T had been done questionless; the ugliest creature
Creation fram'd for some use, yet to see
I could not mark so much where it should be!

ALSEMERO. Lady –

BEATRICE [*aside*]. Why, men of art make much of poison,
Keep one to expel another; where was my art?

ALSEMERO. Lady, you hear not me.

BEATRICE.   I do especially, sir;
The present times are not so sure of our side
As those hereafter may be; we must use 'em then.   50
As thrifty folks their wealth, sparingly now,
Till the time opens.

ALSEMERO.   You teach wisdom, lady.

BEATRICE. Within there – Diaphanta!

Enter DIAPHANTA.

DIAPHANTA.   Do you call, madam?

BEATRICE. Perfect your service, and conduct this gentleman
    The private way you brought him.

DIAPHANTA.   I shall, madam.

ALSEMERO. My love's as firm as love e'er built upon.

Exeunt DIAPHANTA *and* ALSEMERO. *Enter* DE FLORES.

DE FLORES [*aside*]. I have watch'd this meeting and do
        wonder much
    What shall become of tother; I'm sure both
    Cannot be serv'd unless she transgress; happily
    Then I'll put in for one: for if a woman   60
    Fly from one point, from him she makes a husband,
    She spreads and mounts then like arithmetic,
    One, ten, a hundred, a thousand, ten thousand,
    Proves in time sutler to an army royal.
    Now do I look to be most richly rail'd at,
    Yet I must see her.

BEATRICE [*aside*].   Why, put case I loath'd him
    As much as youth and beauty hates a sepulchre,
    Must I needs show it? Cannot I keep that secret,
    And serve my turn upon him? See, he's here. –
    De Flores!

DE FLORES [*aside*]. Ha, I shall run mad with joy;   70
    She call'd me fairly by my name De Flores,
    And neither rogue nor rascal!

BEATRICE.   What ha' you done
   To your face a-late? Y'have met with some good physician;
   Y'have prun'd yourself methinks, you were not wont
   To look so amorously.

DE FLORES [*aside*].   Not I;
   'Tis the same physnomy, to a hair and pimple,
   Which she call'd scurvy scarce an hour ago:
   How is this?

BEATRICE.   Come hither; nearer man!

DE FLORES [*aside*]. I'm up to the chin in heaven.

BEATRICE.   Turn, let me see;
   Faugh, 'tis but the heat of the liver, I perceiv't.   80
   I thought it had been worse.

DE FLORES [*aside*].   Her fingers touch'd me!
   She smells all amber.

BEATRICE. I'll make a water for you shall cleanse this
   Within a fortnight.

DE FLORES.   With your own hands, lady?

BEATRICE. Yes, mine own, sir; in a work of cure
   I'll trust no other.

DE FLORES [*aside*]. 'Tis half an act of pleasure
   To hear her talk thus to me.

BEATRICE.   When w'are us'd
   To a hard face, 'tis not so unpleasing;
   It mends still in opinion, hourly mends,
   I see it by experience.

DE FLORES [*aside*].   I was blest.   90
   To light upon this minute; I'll make use on't.

BEATRICE. Hardness becomes the visage of a man well,
   It argues service, resolution, manhood,
   If cause were of employment.

DE FLORES.   'Twould be soon seen,
   If e'er your ladyship had cause to use it.
   I would but wish the honour of a service
   So happy as that mounts to.

BEATRICE.   We shall try you –
   O my De Flores!

DE FLORES [*aside*]. How's that?
   She calls me hers already, 'my De Flores'! –
   You were about to sigh out somewhat, madam.   100

BEATRICE. No, was I? I forgot – O!

DE FLORES.   There 'tis again –
   The very fellow on't.

BEATRICE.   You are too quick, sir.

DE FLORES. There's no excuse for't now, I heard it twice,
   madam.
   That sigh would fain have utterance, take pity on't,
   And lend it a free word; 'las, how it labours
   For liberty! I hear the murmur yet
   Beat at your bosom.

BEATRICE.   Would creation –

DE FLORES [*aside*]. Ay, well said, that's it.

BEATRICE.   Had form'd me man!

DE FLORES [*aside*]. Nay, that's not it.

BEATRICE.   O, 'tis the soul of freedom!.
   I should not then be forc'd to marry one   110

I hate beyond all depths, I should have power
Then to oppose my loathings, nay, remove 'em
Forever from my sight.

DE FLORES [*aside*].   O blest occasion! –
You, without change to your sex, you have your wishes.
Claim so much man in me.

BEATRICE.   In thee, De Flores?
There's small cause for that.

DE FLORES.   Put it not from me,
It's a service that I kneel for to you.

[*Kneels.*]

BEATRICE. You are too violent to mean faithfully;
There's horror in my service, blood and danger;
Can those be things to sue for?

DE FLORES.   If you knew   120
How sweet it were to me to be employed
In any act of yours, you would say then
I fail'd, and us'd not reverence enough
When I receive the charge on't.

BEATRICE [*aside*].   This is much, methinks;
Belike his wants are greedy, and to such
Gold tastes like angels' food. – Rise.

DE FLORES. I'll have the work first.

BEATRICE [*aside*].   Possible his need
Is strong upon him. [*Gives him money.*] There's to
     encourage thee:
As thou art forward and thy service dangerous,
Thy reward shall be precious.   129

DE FLORES.   That I have thought on;
I have assur'd myself of that beforehand

And know it will be precious; the thought ravishes.

BEATRICE. Then take him to thy fury!

DE FLORES.   I thirst for him.

BEATRICE. Alonzo de Piracquo!

DE FLORES.   His end's upon him;
    He shall be seen no more.

BEATRICE. How lovely now dost thou appear to me!
    Never was man dearlier rewarded.

DE FLORES. I do think of that.

BEATRICE. Be wondrous careful in the execution.

DE FLORES. Why, are not both our lives upon the cast?   140

BEATRICE. Then I throw all my fears upon thy service.

DE FLORES. They ne'er shall rise to hurt you.

BEATRICE.   When the deed's done,
    I'll furnish thee with all things for thy flight;
    Thou may'st live bravely in another country.

DE FLORES. Ay, ay, we'll talk of that hereafter.

BEATRICE [aside].   I shall rid myself
    Of two inveterate loathings at one time,
    Piracquo, and his dog-face.

    Exit.

DE FLORES.   O my blood!
    Methinks I feel her in mine arms already,
    Her wanton fingers combing out this beard,
    And being pleased, praising this bad face.   150
    Hunger and pleasure, they'll commend sometimes

Slovenly dishes, and feed heartily on 'em,
Nay, which is stranger, refuse daintier for 'em.
Some women are odd feeders – I'm too loud.
Here comes the man goes supperless to bed,
Yet shall not rise tomorrow to his dinner.

Enter ALONZO.

ALONZO. De Flores.

DE FLORES.   My kind, honourable lord.

ALONZO. I am glad I ha' met with thee.

DE FLORES.   Sir.

ALONZO.   Thou canst show me
The full strength of the castle?

DE FLORES.   That I can, sir.

ALONZO. I much desire it.

DE FLORES.   And if the ways and straits   160
Of some of the passages be not too tedious for you,
I will assure you, worth your time and sight, my lord.

ALONZO. Puh! That shall be no hindrance.

DE FLORES.   I'm your servant, then:
'Tis now near dinner time; 'gainst your lordship's rising
I'll have the keys about me.

ALONZO.   Thanks, kind De Flores.

DE FLORES [*aside*]. He's safely thrust upon me beyond hopes.

Exeunt.

ACT THREE

[Scene i]

Enter ALONZO *and* DE FLORES. (*In the act-time* DE FLORES *hides a naked rapier.*)

DE FLORES. Yes, here are all the keys; I was afraid, my lord,
    I'd wanted for the postern, this is it.
    I've all, I've all, my lord: this for the sconce.

ALONZO. 'Tis a most spacious and impregnable fort.

DE FLORES. You'll tell me more, my lord: this descent
    Is somewhat narrow, we shall never pass
    Well with our weapons, they'll but trouble us.

ALONZO. Thou say'st true.

DE FLORES.   Pray let me help your lordship.

ALONZO. 'Tis done. Thanks, kind De Flores.

DE FLORES.   Here are hooks, my lord,
    To hang such things on purpose.   10

    [*Hangs up the swords.*]

ALONZO.   Lead, I'll follow thee.

    Exeunt at one door and enter at the other.

[Scene ii]

DE FLORES. All this is nothing; you shall see anon
  A place you little dream on.

ALONZO.   I am glad
  I have this leisure: all your master's house
  Imagine I ha' taken a gondola.

DE FLORES. All but myself, sir, [*Aside.*] which makes up
    my safety.
  My lord, I'll place you at a casement here
  Will show you the full strength of all the castle.
  Look, spend your eye awhile upon that object.

ALONZO. Here's rich variety, De Flores.

DE FLORES.   Yes, sir.

ALONZO. Goodly munition.   10

DE FLORES.   Ay, there's ordnance, sir,
  No bastard metal, will ring you a peal like bells
  At great men's funerals; keep your eye straight, my lord,
  Take special notice of that sconce before you,
  There you may dwell awhile.

ALONZO.   I am upon't.

DE FLORES. And so am I.

  [*Stabs him with the hidden rapier.*]

ALONZO.   De Flores! O De Flores,
  Whose malice hast thou put on?

DE FLORES.   Do you question
  A work of secrecy? I must silence you.

  [*Stabs him.*]

ALONZO. O, O, O.

DE FLORES.   I must silence you.

[Stabs him.]

So, here's an undertaking well accomplish'd.   20
This vault serves to good use now. Ha! what's that
Threw sparkles in my eye? O 'tis a diamond
He wears upon his finger: it was well found,
This will approve the work. What, so fast on?
Not part in death? I'll take a speedy course then,
Finger and all shall off. *[Cuts off the finger.]* So, now I'll clear
The passages from all suspect or fear.

Exit with body.

[Scene iii]

Enter ISABELLA *and* LOLLIO.

ISABELLA. Why, sirrah? Whence have you commission
To fetter the doors against me?
If you keep me in a cage, pray whistle to me,
Let me be doing something.

LOLLIO. You shall be doing, if it please you; I'll whistle to
you if you'll pipe after.

ISABELLA. Is it your master's pleasure, or your own,
To keep me in this pinfold?

LOLLIO. 'Tis for my master's pleasure, lest being taken
in another man's corn, you might be pounded in
another place.   10

ISABELLA. 'Tis very well, and he'll prove very wise.

LOLLIO. He says you have company enough in the house,
if you please to be sociable, of all sorts of people.

ISABELLA. Of all sorts? Why, here's none but fools and
madmen.

LOLLIO. Very well: and where will you find any other, if you
should go abroad? There's my master and I to boot too.

ISABELLA. Of either sort one, a madman and a fool.

LOLLIO. I would ev'n participate of both then, if I were as
you; I know y'are half mad already, be half foolish too.

ISABELLA. Y'are a brave saucy rascal! Come on, sir,   20
Afford me then the pleasure of your bedlam;
You were commending once today to me
Your last-come lunatic, what a proper
Body there was without brains to guide it,
And what a pitiful delight appear'd
In that defect, as if your wisdom had found
A mirth in madness; pray, sir, let me partake,
If there be such a pleasure.

LOLLIO. If I do not show you the handsomest, discreetest
madman, one that I may call the understanding madman,
then say I am a fool.   30

ISABELLA. Well, a match, I will say so.

LOLLIO. When you have a taste of the madman, you shall, if
you please, see Fools' College, o'th'side; I seldom lock there,
'tis but shooting a bolt or two, and you are amongst 'em.

Exit.

Enter presently.

Come on, sir, let me see how handsomely you'll behave
yourself now.

Enter FRANCISCUS.

FRANCISCUS. How sweetly she looks! O but there's a wrinkle
in her brow as deep as philosophy; Anacreon, drink to my
mistress's health, I'll pledge it: stay, stay, there's a spider in
the cup! No, 'tis but a grapestone, swallow it, fear nothing,
poet; so, so, lift higher. 40

ISABELLA. Alack, alack, 'tis too full of pity
To be laugh'd at; how fell he mad? Canst thou tell?

LOLLIO. For love, mistress: he was a pretty poet too, and that
set him forwards first; the Muses then forsook him, he ran
mad for a chambermaid, yet she was but a dwarf neither.

FRANCISCUS. Hail, bright Titania!
Why stand'st thou idle on these flow'ry banks?
Oberon is dancing with his Dryades;
I'll gather daisies, primrose, violets,
And bind them in a verse of poesy. 50

LOLLIO. Not too near; you see your danger.

[*Shows the whip.*]

FRANCISCUS. O hold thy hand, great Diomed,
Thou feed'st thy horses well, they shall obey thee;
Get up, Bucephalus kneels.

[*Kneels.*]

LOLLIO. You see how I awe my flock; a shepherd has not his
dog at more obedience.

ISABELLA. His conscience is unquiet, sure that was
The cause of this. A proper gentleman.

FRANCISCUS. Come hither, Esculapius; hide the poison.

[LOLLIO *hides his whip.*]

LOLLIO. Well, 'tis hid.   60

FRANCISCUS. Didst thou never hear of one Tiresias, a
    famous poet?

LOLLIO. Yes, that kept tame wild-geese.

FRANCISCUS. That's he; I am the man.

LOLLIO. No!

FRANCISCUS. Yes, but make no words on't, I was a man
    seven years ago.

LOLLIO. A stripling I think you might.

FRANCISCUS. Now I'm a woman, all feminine.

LOLLIO. I would I might see that.

FRANCISCUS. Juno struck me blind.

LOLLIO. I'll ne'er believe that; for a woman, they say, has
    an eye more than a man.   70

FRANCISCUS. I say she struck me blind.

LOLLIO. And Luna made you mad; you have two trades to
    beg with.

FRANCISCUS. Luna is now big-bellied, and there's room
    For both of us to ride with Hecate;
    I'll drag thee up into her silver sphere,
    And there we'll kick the dog, and beat the bush,
    That barks against the witches of the night:
    The swift lycanthropi that walks the round,
    We'll tear their wolvish skins and save the sheep.

[*Tries to seize* LOLLIO.]

LOLLIO. Is't come to this? Nay, then my poison comes forth
again. [*Flourishes whip.*] Mad slave, indeed, abuse your
keeper!

ISABELLA. I prithee hence with him, now he grows
dangerous.

FRANCISCUS (*sings*).
Sweet love, pity me,
Give me leave to lie with thee.

LOLLIO. No, I'll see you wiser first: to your own kennel.

FRANCISCUS. No noise, she sleeps, draw all the curtains
round;
Let no soft sound molest the pretty soul
But love, and love creeps in at a mouse-hole.

LOLLIO. I would you would get into your hole.

Exit FRANCISCUS.

Now, mistress, I will bring you another sort, you shall be
fool'd another while; Tony, come hither Tony; look who's
yonder, Tony.

Enter ANTONIO.

ANTONIO. Cousin, is it not my aunt?

LOLLIO. Yes, 'tis one of 'em, Tony.

ANTONIO. He, he! How do you, uncle?

LOLLIO. Fear him not mistress, 'tis a gentle nigget; you may
play with him, as safely with him as with his bauble.

ISABELLA. How long hast thou been a fool?

ANTONIO. Ever since I came hither, cousin.

ISABELLA. Cousin? I'm none of thy cousins, fool.   100

LOLLIO. O mistress, fools have always so much wit as to
   claim their kindred.

MADMAN (*within*). Bounce, bounce, he falls, he falls!

ISABELLA. Hark you, your scholars in the upper room are out
   of order.

LOLLIO [*shouts*]. Must I come amongst you there? – Keep you
   the fool, mistress; I'll go up and play left-handed Orlando
   amongst the madmen.

   Exit.

ISABELLA. Well, sir.

ANTONIO. 'Tis opportuneful now, sweet lady! Nay,
   Cast no amazing eye upon this change.

ISABELLA. Ha!   110

ANTONIO. This shape of folly shrouds your dearest love,
   The truest servant to your powerful beauties,
   Whose magic had this force thus to transform me.

ISABELLA. You are a fine fool indeed.

ANTONIO.   O 'tis not strange:
   Love has an intellect that runs through all
   The scrutinous sciences, and like
   A cunning poet, catches a quantity
   Of every knowledge, yet brings all home
   Into one mystery, into one secret
   That he proceeds in.

ISABELLA.   Y'are a parlous fool.   120

ANTONIO. No danger in me: I bring nought but love
   And his soft-wounding shafts to strike you with:
   Try but one arrow; if it hurt you,
   I'll stand you twenty back in recompense.

ISABELLA. A forward fool too!

ANTONIO.   This was love's teaching:
   A thousand ways he fashion'd out my way,
   And this I found the safest and nearest
   To tread the Galaxia to my star.

ISABELLA. Profound, withal! Certain, you dream'd of this;
   Love never taught it waking.

ANTONIO.   Take no acquaintance
   Of these outward follies; there is within   130
   A gentleman that loves you.

ISABELLA.   When I see him
   I'll speak with him; so in the meantime keep
   Your habit, it becomes you well enough.
   As you are a gentleman, I'll not discover you;
   That's all the favour that you must expect:
   When you are weary, you may leave the school,
   For all this while you have but play'd the fool.

Enter LOLLIO.

ANTONIO [*aside*]. And must again; he, he! I thank you,
   cousin;
   I'll be your valentine tomorrow morning.

LOLLIO. How do you like the fool, mistress?   140

ISABELLA. Passing well, sir.

LOLLIO. Is he not witty, pretty well for a fool?

ISABELLA. If he hold on as he begins, he is like to come to
something.

LOLLIO. Ay, thank a good tutor: you may put him to't; he
begins to answer pretty hard questions. Tony, how many is
five times six?

ANTONIO. Five times six, is six times five.

LOLLIO. What arithmetician could have answer'd better? How
many is one hundred and seven?

ANTONIO. One hundred and seven, is seven hundred and
one, cousin.

LOLLIO. This is no wit to speak on; will you be rid of the
fool now?   150

ISABELLA. By no means, let him stay a little.

MADMAN (*within*). Catch there, catch the last couple in hell!

LOLLIO [*shouts*]. Again? Must I come amongst you? Would
my master were come home! I am not able to govern both
these wards together.

Exit.

ANTONIO. Why should a minute of love's hour be lost?

ISABELLA. Fie, out again' I had rather you kept
Your other posture: you become not your tongue
When you speak from your clothes.

ANTONIO.   How can he freeze,
Lives near so sweet a warmth? Shall I alone
Walk through the orchard of the Hesperides   160
And cowardly not dare to pull an apple?
This with the red cheeks I must venture for.

[*Tries to kiss her.*]

Enter LOLLIO *above.*

ISABELLA. Take heed, there's giants keep 'em.

LOLLIO [*aside*]. How now, fool, are you good at that? Have
    you read Lipsius? He's past *Ars Amandi;* I believe I must put
    harder questions to him, I perceive that.

ISABELLA. You are bold without fear too.

ANTONIO.   What should I fear,
    Having all joys about me? Do you smile,
    And love shall play the wanton on your lip,   170
    Meet and retire, retire and meet again:
    Look you but cheerfully, and in your eyes
    I shall behold mine own deformity
    And dress myself up fairer; I know this shape
    Becomes me not, but in those bright mirrors
    I shall array me handsomely.

LOLLIO [*aside*].   Cuckoo, cuckoo!

Exit.

[*Enter*] MADMEN *above, some as birds, others as beasts.*

ANTONIO. What are these?

ISABELLA.   Of fear enough to part us;
    Yet are they but our schools of lunatics,
    That act their fantasies in any shapes
    Suiting their present thoughts; if sad, they cry;   180
    If mirth be their conceit, they laugh again.
    Sometimes they imitate the beasts and birds,
    Singing, or howling, braying, barking; all
    As their wild fancies prompt 'em.

[*Exeunt* MADMEN.]

Enter LOLLIO.

ANTONIO.   These are no fears.

ISABELLA. But here's a large one, my man.

ANTONIO. Ha, he! That's fine sport indeed, cousin.

LOLLIO. I would my master were come home, 'tis too much
    for one shepherd to govern two of these flocks; nor can
    I believe that one churchman can instruct two benefices
    at once; there will be some incurable mad of the one side,
    and very fools on the other. Come, Tony.

ANTONIO. Prithee, cousin, let me stay here still.   190

LOLLIO. No, you must to your book now you have play'd
    sufficiently.

ISABELLA. Your fool is grown wondrous witty.

LOLLIO. Well, I'll say nothing; but I do not think but he will
    put you down one of these days.

    Exeunt LOLLIO *and* ANTONIO.

ISABELLA. Here the restrained current might make breach,
    Spite of the watchful bankers; would a woman stray,
    She need not gad abroad to seek her sin,
    It would be brought home one ways or other:
    The needle's point will to the fixed north,
    Such drawing arctics women's beauties are.   200

    Enter LOLLIO.

LOLLIO. How dost thou, sweet rogue?

ISABELLA. How now?

LOLLIO. Come, there are degrees, one fool may be better
than another.

ISABELLA. What's the matter?

LOLLIO. Nay, if thou giv'st thy mind to fool's-flesh, have at
thee!

[*Tries to kiss her.*]

ISABELLA. You bold slave, you!

LOLLIO. I could follow now as tother fool did:

'What should I fear,
Having all joys about me? Do you but smile,
And love shall play the wanton on your lip,   210
Meet and retire, retire and meet again:
Look you but cheerfully, and in your eyes
I shall behold my own deformity,
And dress myself up fairer; I know this shape
Becomes me not – '

and so as it follows; but is not this the more foolish way?
Come, sweet rogue; kiss me, my little Lacedemonian. Let me
feel how thy pulses beat; thou hast a thing about thee would
do a man pleasure, I'll lay my hand on't.   220

ISABELLA. Sirrah, no more! I see you have discovered
This love's knight-errant, who hath made adventure
For purchase of my love; be silent, mute,
Mute as a statue, or his injunction
For me enjoying, shall be to cut thy throat:
I'll do it, though for no other purpose,
And be sure he'll not refuse it.

LOLLIO. My share, that's all; I'll have my fool's part with you.

ISABELLA. No more! Your master.

Enter ALIBIUS.

ALIBIUS.   Sweet, how dost thou?

ISABELLA. Your bounden servant, sir.

ALIBIUS.   Fie, fie, sweetheart,
No more of that.   230

ISABELLA.   You were best lock me up.

ALIBIUS. In my arms and bosom, my sweet Isabella,
I'll lock thee up most nearly. Lollio,
We have employment, we have task in hand;
At noble Vermandero's, our castle-captain,
There is a nuptial to be solemniz'd,
Beatrice-Joanna, his fair daughter, bride,
For which the gentleman hath bespoke our pains:
A mixture of our madmen and our fools
To finish, as it were, and make the fag   240
Of all the revels, the third night from the first;
Only an unexpected passage over,
To make a frightful pleasure, that is all,
But not the all I aim at; could we so act it,
To teach it in a wild distracted measure,
Though out of form and figure, breaking time's head,
It were no matter, 'twould be heal'd again
In one age or other, if not in this.
This, this, Lollio, there's a good reward begun,
And will beget a bounty, be it known.   250

LOLLIO. This is easy, sir, I'll warrant you: you have about you
fools and madmen that can dance very well; and 'tis no
wonder, your best dancers are not the wisest men; the
reason is, with often jumping they jolt their brains down into
their feet, that their wits lie more in their heels than in their
heads.

ALIBIUS. Honest Lollio, thou giv'st me a good reason,
And a comfort in it.

ISABELLA.   Y'have a fine trade on't,
Madmen and fools are a staple commodity.

ALIBIUS. O wife, we must eat, wear clothes, and live.
Just at the lawyers' haven we arrive,
By madmen and by fools we both do thrive.   260

Exeunt.

[Scene iv]

Enter VERMANDERO, ALSEMERO, JASPERINO, *and*
BEATRICE.

VERMANDERO. Valencia speaks so nobly of you, sir,
I wish I had a daughter now for you.

ALSEMERO. The fellow of this creature were a partner
For a king's love.

VERMANDERO.   I had her fellow once, sir,
But heaven has married her to joys eternal;
'Twere sin to wish her in this vale again.
Come, sir, your friend and you shall see the pleasures
Which my health chiefly joys in.

ALSEMERO. I hear the beauty of this seat largely.

VERMANDERO. It falls much short of that.   9

Exeunt. Manet BEATRICE.

BEATRICE.   So, here's one step
Into my father's favour; time will fix him.

I have got him now the liberty of the house:
So wisdom by degrees works out her freedom;
And if that eye be dark'ned that offends me
(I wait but that eclipse) this gentleman
Shall soon shine glorious in my father's liking,
Through the refulgent virtue of my love.

Enter DE FLORES.

DE FLORES [*aside*]. My thoughts are at a banquet for
    the deed,
  I feel no weight in't, 'tis but light and cheap   20
For the sweet recompense that I set down for't.

BEATRICE. De Flores.

DE FLORES.   Lady.

BEATRICE.   Thy looks promise cheerfully.

DE FLORES. All things are answerable, time, circumstance,
  Your wishes, and my service.

BEATRICE.   Is it done then?

DE FLORES. Piracquo is no more.

BEATRICE. My joys start at mine eyes; our sweet'st delights
  Are evermore born weeping.

DE FLORES.   I've a token for you.

BEATRICE. For me?

DE FLORES.   But it was sent somewhat unwillingly,
  I could not get the ring without the finger.

  [*Shows the severed finger.*]

BEATRICE. Bless me! What hast thou done?   29

DE FLORES.   Why, is that more
  Than killing the whole man? I cut his heart-strings.
  A greedy hand thrust in a dish at court
  In a mistake hath had as much as this.

BEATRICE. 'Tis the first token my father made me send him.

DE FLORES. And I made him send it back again
  For his last token; I was loath to leave it,
  And I'm sure dead men have no use of jewels.
  He was as loath to part with't, for it stuck
  As if the flesh and it were both one substance.

BEATRICE. At the stag's fall the keeper has his fees: 40
  'Tis soon applied, all dead men's fees are yours, sir;
  I pray, bury the finger, but the stone
  You may make use on shortly; the true value,
  Take't of my truth, is near three hundred ducats.

DE FLORES. 'Twill hardly buy a capcase for one's
        conscience, though,
  To keep it from the worm, as fine as 'tis.
  Well, being my fees I'll take it;
  Great men have taught me that, or else my merit
  Would scorn the way on't.

BEATRICE.   It might justly, sir:
  Why, thou mistak'st, De Flores, 'tis not given
  In state of recompense.

DE FLORES.   No, I hope so, lady,   50
  You should soon witness my contempt to't then!

BEATRICE. Prithee, thou look'st as if thou wert offended.

DE FLORES. That were strange, lady; 'tis not possible
  My service should draw such a cause from you.
  Offended? Could you think so? That were much

For one of my performance, and so warm
Yet in my service.

BEATRICE. 'Twere misery in me to give you cause, sir.

DE FLORES. I know so much, it were so, misery
In her most sharp condition.

BEATRICE.   'Tis resolv'd then;   60
Look you, sir, here's three thousand golden florins:
I have not meanly thought upon thy merit.

DE FLORES. What, salary? Now you move me.

BEATRICE.   How, De Flores?

DE FLORES. Do you place me in the rank of verminous
    fellows,
To destroy things for wages? Offer gold?
The life blood of man! Is anything
Valued too precious for my recompense?

BEATRICE. I understand thee not.

DE FLORES.   I could ha' hir'd
A journeyman in murder at this rate,
And mine own conscience might have [slept at ease]   70
And have had the work brought home.

BEATRICE [*aside*].   I'm in a labyrinth;
What will content him? I would fain be rid of him.
I'll double the sum, sir.

DE FLORES.   You take a course
To double my vexation, that's the good you do.

BEATRICE [*aside*]. Bless me! I am now in worse plight
    than I was;
I know not what will please him: For my fear's sake,

I prithee make away with all speed possible.
And if thou be'st so modest not to name
The sum that will content thee, paper blushes not;   80
Send thy demand in writing, it shall follow thee,
But prithee take thy flight.

DE FLORES.   You must fly too then.

BEATRICE. I?

DE FLORES. I'll not stir a foot else.

BEATRICE.   What's your meaning?

DE FLORES. Why, are not you as guilty, in, I'm sure,
    As deep as I? And we should stick together.
    Come, your fears counsel you but ill, my absence
    Would draw suspect upon you instantly;
    There were no rescue for you.

BEATRICE [*aside*].   He speaks home.

DE FLORES. Nor is it fit we two, engag'd so jointly,
    Should part and live asunder.

    [*Tries to kiss her.*]

BEATRICE.   How now, sir?
    This shows not well.   90

DE FLORES.   What makes your lip so strange?
    This must not be betwixt us.

BEATRICE [*aside*].   The man talks wildly.

DE FLORES. Come, kiss me with a zeal now.

BEATRICE [*aside*].   Heaven, I doubt him!

DE FLORES. I will not stand so long to beg 'em shortly.

BEATRICE. Take heed, De Flores, of forgetfulness,
　'Twill soon betray us.

DE FLORES.　　　　　Take you heed first;
　Faith, y'are grown much forgetful, y'are to blame in't.

BEATRICE [aside]. He's bold, and I am blam'd for't!

DE FLORES.　　　　　　　　　I have eas'd you
　Of your trouble, think on't, I'm in pain,
　And must be eas'd of you; 'tis a charity,　　　　100
　Justice invites your blood to understand me.

BEATRICE. I dare not.

DE FLORES.　　　Quickly!

BEATRICE.　　　　O I never shall!
　Speak it yet further off that I may lose
　What has been spoken, and no sound remain on't.
　I would not hear so much offence again
　For such another deed.

DE FLORES.　　　　Soft, lady, soft;
　The last is not yet paid for. O this act
　Has put me into spirit; I was as greedy on't
　As the parch'd earth of moisture, when the clouds weep.
　Did you not mark, I wrought myself into't,　　　　109
　Nay, sued and kneel'd for't: why was all that pains took?
　You see I have thrown contempt upon your gold,
　Not that I want it [not], for I do piteously:
　In order I will come unto't, and make use on't,
　But 'twas not held so precious to begin with;
　For I place wealth after the heels of pleasure,
　And were I not resolv'd in my belief
　That thy virginity were perfect in thee,
　I should but take my recompense with grudging,
　As if I had but half my hopes I agreed for.　　　　119

BEATRICE. Why, 'tis impossible thou canst be so wicked,
　　Or shelter such a cunning cruelty,
　　To make his death the murderer of my honour!
　　Thy language is so bold and vicious,
　　I cannot see which way I can forgive it
　　With any modesty.

DE FLORES.　　　　Push, you forget yourself!
　　A woman dipp'd in blood, and talk of modesty?

BEATRICE. O misery of sin! Would I had been bound
　　Perpetually unto my living hate
　　In that Piracquo, than to hear these words.
　　Think but upon the distance that creation　　　　130
　　Set 'twixt thy blood and mine, and keep thee there.

DE FLORES. Look but into your conscience, read me there,
　　'Tis a true book, you'll find me there your equal.
　　Push! Fly not to your birth, but settle you
　　In what the act has made you, y'are no more now,
　　You must forget your parentage to me:
　　Y'are the deed's creature; by that name
　　You lost your first condition, and I challenge you,
　　As peace and innocency has turn'd you out,
　　And made you one with me.　　　　140

BEATRICE.　　　　With thee, foul villain?

DE FLORES. Yes, my fair murd'ress; do you urge me?
　　Though thou writ'st maid, thou whore in thy affection!
　　'Twas chang'd from thy first love, and that's a kind
　　Of whoredom in thy heart; and he's chang'd now,
　　To bring thy second on, thy Alsemero,
　　Whom, by all sweets that ever darkness tasted,
　　If I enjoy thee not, thou ne'er enjoy'st;
　　I'll blast the hopes and joys of marriage,
　　I'll confess all; my life I rate at nothing　　　　150

BEATRICE. De Flores!

DE FLORES. I shall rest from all lovers' plagues then;
   I live in pain now: that shooting eye
   Will burn my heart to cinders.

BEATRICE.   O sir, hear me.

DE FLORES. She that in life and love refuses me,
   In death and shame my partner she shall be.

BEATRICE. Stay, hear me once for all; [*Kneels.*] I make
      thee master
   Of all the wealth I have in gold and jewels:
   Let me go poor unto my bed with honour,
   And I am rich in all things.

DE FLORES.   Let this silence thee: 160
   The wealth of all Valencia shall not buy
   My pleasure from me;
   Can you weep Fate from its determin'd purpose?
   So soon may [you] weep me.

BEATRICE.   Vengeance begins;
   Murder I see is followed by more sins.
   Was my creation in the womb so curs'd,
   It must engender with a viper first?

DE FLORES. Come, rise, and shroud your blushes in
      my bosom;

   [*Raises her.*]

   Silence is one of pleasure's best receipts:
   Thy peace is wrought for ever in this yielding.   170
   'Las, how the turtle pants! Thou'lt love anon
   What thou so fear'st and faint'st to venture on.

   Exeunt.

ACT FOUR

[Scene i]

[*Dumb show.*]

Enter GENTLEMEN, VERMANDERO *meeting them with action of wonderment at the flight of* PIRACQUO. *Enter* ALSEMERO, *with* JASPERINO, *and* GALLANTS; VERMANDERO *points to him, the* GENTLEMEN *seeming to applaud the choice.* [*Exeunt in procession* VERMANDERO] ALSEMERO, JASPERINO, *and* GENTLE-MEN; BEATRICE *the bride following in great state, accompanied with* DIAPHANTA, ISABELLA *and other* GENTLEWOMEN; DE FLORES *after all, smiling at the accident;* ALONZO'S GHOST *appears to* DE FLORES *in the midst of his smile, startles him, showing him the hand whose finger he had cut off. They pass over in great solemnity.*

Enter BEATRICE.

BEATRICE. This fellow has undone me endlessly,
   Never was bride so fearfully distress'd,.
   The more I think upon th'ensuing night
   And whom I am to cope with in embraces,
   One that's ennobled both in blood and mind,
   So clear in understanding (that's my plague now)
   Before whose judgment will my fault appear
   Like malefactors' crimes before tribunals;
   There is no hiding on't, the more I dive
   Into my own distress; how a wise man   10
   Stands for a great calamity! There's no venturing
   Into his bed, what course soe'er I light upon,

Without my shame, which may grow up to danger;
He cannot but in justice strangle me
As I lie by him, as a cheater use me;
'Tis a precious craft to play with a false die
Before a cunning gamester. Here's his closet,
The key left in't, and he abroad i'th'park:
Sure 'twas forgot; I'll be so bold as look in't.

[*Opens closet.*]

Bless me! A right physician's closet 'tis,   20
Set round with vials, every one her mark too.
Sure he does practise physic for his own use,
Which may be safely call'd your great man's wisdom.
What manuscript lies here? 'The Book of Experiment,
Call'd Secrets in Nature'; so 'tis, 'tis so;
'How to know whether a woman be with child or no'.
I hope I am not yet; if he should try though!
Let me see, folio forty-five. Here 'tis;
The leaf tuck'd down upon't, the place suspicious.

'If you would know whether a woman be with child or   30
not, give her two spoonfuls of the white water in glass C . . .'

Where's that glass C? O yonder, I see't now:

'. . . and if she be with child, she sleeps full twelve hours
after, if not, not.'

None of that water comes into my belly.
I'll know you from a hundred; I could break you now,
Or turn you into milk, and so beguile
The master of the mystery, but I'll look to you.
Ha! That which is next is ten times worse.
'How to know whether a woman be a maid or not';   40
If that should be applied, what would become of me?
Belike he has a strong faith of my purity,

That never yet made proof; but this he calls

'A merry sleight, but true experiment, the author Antonius
Mizaldus. Give the party you suspect the quantity of a
spoonful of the water in the glass M, which upon her that
is a maid makes three several effects: 'twill make her
incontinently gape, then fall into a sudden sneezing, last
into a violent laughing; else dull, heavy, and lumpish.'

Where had I been?   50
I fear it, yet 'tis seven hours to bedtime.

Enter DIAPHANTA.

DIAPHANTA. Cuds, madam, are you here?

BEATRICE [*aside*].   Seeing that wench now,
A trick comes in my mind; 'tis a nice piece
Gold cannot purchase; I come hither, wench,
To look my lord.

DIAPHANTA [*aside*]. Would I had such a cause to look
       him too!
Why, he's i'th'park, madam.

BEATRICE. There let him be.

DIAPHANTA.   Ay, madam, let him compass
Whole parks and forests, as great rangers do;
At roosting time a little lodge can hold 'em.
Earth-conquering Alexander, that thought the world
Too narrow for him, in the end had but his pit-hole.   60

BEATRICE. I fear thou art not modest, Diaphanta.

DIAPHANTA. Your thoughts are so unwilling to be known,
       madam;
'Tis ever the bride's fashion towards bedtime
To set light by her joys, as if she ow'd 'em not.

BEATRICE. Her joys? Her fears, thou would'st say.

DIAPHANTA.   Fear of what?

BEATRICE. Art thou a maid, and talk'st so to a maid?
  You leave a blushing business behind,
  Beshrew your heart for't!

DIAPHANTA.   Do you mean good sooth, madam?

BEATRICE. Well, if I'd thought upon the fear at first,   70
  Man should have been unknown.

DIAPHANTA.   Is't possible?

BEATRICE. I will give a thousand ducats to that woman
  Would try what my fear were, and tell me true
  Tomorrow, when she gets from't; as she likes
  I might perhaps be drawn to't.

DIAPHANTA.   Are you in earnest?

BEATRICE. Do you get the woman, then challenge me,
  And see if I'll fly from't; but I must tell you
  This by the way, she must be a true maid,
  Else there's no trial, my fears are not hers else.

DIAPHANTA. Nay, she that I would put into your hands,
    madam,   80
  Shall be a maid.

BEATRICE.   You know I should be sham'd else,
  Because she lies for me.

DIAPHANTA.   'Tis a strange humour;
  But are you serious still? Would you resign
  Your first night's pleasure, and give money too?

BEATRICE. As willingly as live. [*Aside.*] Alas, the gold
  Is but a by-bet to wedge in the honour.

DIAPHANTA. I do not know how the world goes abroad
　　For faith or honesty, there's both requir'd in this.
　　Madam, what say you to me, and stray no further?
　　I've a good mind, in troth, to earn your money. 90

BEATRICE. Y'are too quick, I fear, to be a maid.

DIAPHANTA. How? Not a maid? Nay, then you urge me, madam;
　　Your honourable self is not a truer
　　With all your fears upon you –

BEATRICE [aside].　　　　　　Bad enough then.

DIAPHANTA. Than I with all my lightsome joys about me.

BEATRICE. I'm glad to hear't then; you dare put your honesty
　　Upon an easy trial?

DIAPHANTA.　　　　Easy? – Anything.

BEATRICE. I'll come to you straight.

　　[Goes to closet.]

DIAPHANTA [aside].　　　　She will not search me, will she,
　　Like the forewoman of a female jury? 100

BEATRICE [aside]. Glass M. Ay, this is it; look, Diaphanta,
　　You take no worse than I do. [Drinks.]

DIAPHANTA.　　　　　And in so doing,
　　I will not question what 'tis, but take it. [Drinks.]

BEATRICE [aside]. Now if the experiment be true, 'twill praise itself,
　　And give me noble ease: – begins already;

　　[DIAPHANTA gapes.]

There's the first symptom; and what haste it makes

To fall into the second, there by this time!

[DIAPHANTA *sneezes.*]

Most admirable secret! On the contrary,
It stirs not me a whit, which most concerns it.

DIAPHANTA. Ha, ha, ha!

BEATRICE [*aside*].   Just in all things and in order
As if 'twere circumscrib'd; one accident   110
Gives way unto another.

DIAPHANTA.   Ha, ha, ha!

BEATRICE.   How now, wench?

DIAPHANTA. Ha, ha, ha! I am so, so light at heart – ha, ha,
ha! – so pleasurable!
But one swig more, sweet madam.

BEATRICE.   Ay, tomorrow;
We shall have time to sit by't.

DIAPHANTA.   Now I'm sad again.

BEATRICE [*aside*]. It lays itself so gently, too! Come, wench,
Most honest Diaphanta I dare call thee now.

DIAPHANTA. Pray tell me, madam, what trick call you this?

BEATRICE. I'll tell thee all hereafter; we must study
The carriage of this business.

DIAPHANTA.   I shall carry't well,
Because I love the burthen.

BEATRICE.   About midnight   120
You must not fail to steal forth gently,
That I may use the place.

DIAPHANTA.   O fear not, madam,
   I shall be cool by that time. [*Aside.*] The bride's place,
   And with a thousand ducats! I'm for a Justice now,
   I bring a portion with me; I scorn small fools.

   Exeunt.

[Scene ii]

Enter VERMANDERO *and* SERVANT.

VERMANDERO. I tell thee, knave, mine honour is in question,
   A thing till now free from suspicion,
   Nor ever was there cause. Who of my gentlemen
   Are absent? Tell me and truly how many and who.

SERVANT. Antonio, sir, and Franciscus.

VERMANDERO. When did they leave the castle?

SERVANT. Some ten days since, sir, the one intending to
   Briamata, th'other for Valencia.

VERMANDERO. The time accuses 'em; a charge of murder
   Is brought within my castle gate, Piracquo's murder;   10
   I dare not answer faithfully their absence:
   A strict command of apprehension
   Shall pursue 'em suddenly, and either wipe
   The stain off clear, or openly discover it.
   Provide me winged warrants for the purpose.
   See, I am set on again

   Exit SERVANT.

   Enter TOMAZO.

TOMAZO. I claim a brother of you.

VERMANDERO.   Y'are too hot,
   Seek him not here.

TOMAZO.   Yes, 'mongst your dearest bloods,
   If my peace find no fairer satisfaction;   20
   This is the place must yield account for him,
   For here I left him, and the hasty tie
   Of this snatch'd marriage, gives strong testimony
   Of his most certain ruin.

VERMANDERO.   Certain falsehood!
   This is the place indeed; his breach of faith
   Has too much marr'd both my abused love,
   The honourable love I reserv'd for him,
   And mock'd my daughter's joy; the prepar'd morning
   Blush'd at his infidelity; he left
   Contempt and scorn to throw upon those friends   30
   Whose belief hurt 'em. O 'twas most ignoble
   To take his flight so unexpectedly
   And throw such public wrongs on those that lov'd him.

TOMAZO. Then this is all your answer?

VERMANDERO.   'Tis too fair
   For one of his alliance; and I warn you
   That this place no more see you.

   Enter DE FLORES.

TOMAZO.   The best is,
   There is more ground to meet a man's revenge on.
   Honest De Flores!

DE FLORES.   That's my name indeed.
   Saw you the bride? Good sweet sir, which way took she?

TOMAZO. I have blest mine eyes from seeing such a false one.

DE FLORES [*aside*]. I'd fain get off, this man's not for my
    company, 40
  I smell his brother's blood when I come near him.

TOMAZO. Come hither, kind and true one; I remember
  My brother lov'd thee well.

DE FLORES.   O purely, dear sir!
  [*Aside.*] Methinks I am now again a-killing on him,
  He brings it so fresh to me.

TOMAZO.   Thou canst guess, sirrah
  (One honest friend has an instinct of jealousy),
  At some foul guilty person?

DE FLORES. 'Las, sir, I am so charitable, I think none
  Worse than myself. – You did not see the bride then?

TOMAZO. I prithee name her not. Is she not wicked? 50

DE FLORES. No, no, a pretty, easy, round-pack'd sinner,
  As your most ladies are, else you might think
  I flatter'd her; but, sir, at no hand wicked,
  Till th'are so old their sins and vices meet
  And they salute witches. I am call'd, I think, sir.
  [*Aside.*] His company ev'n o'erlays my conscience.

  Exit.

TOMAZO. That De Flores has a wondrous honest heart;
  He'll bring it out in time, I'm assur'd on't.
  O here's the glorious master of the day's joy.
  'Twill not be long till he and I do reckon. 60

  Enter ALSEMERO.

  Sir!

ALSEMERO. You are most welcome.

TOMAZO.   You may call that word back;
  I do not think I am, nor wish to be.

ALSEMERO. 'Tis strange you found the way to this house
  then.

TOMAZO. Would I'd ne'er known the cause! I'm none of
  those, sir,
  That come to give you joy, and swill your wine;
  'Tis a more precious liquor that must lay
  The fiery thirst I bring.

ALSEMERO.   Your words and you
  Appear to me great strangers.

TOMAZO.   Time and our swords
  May make us more acquainted. This the business: 70
  I should have a brother in your place;
  How treachery and malice have dispos'd of him,
  I'm bound to inquire of him which holds his right,
  Which never could come fairly.

ALSEMERO.   You must look
  To answer for that word, sir.

TOMAZO.   Fear you not,
  I'll have it ready drawn at our next meeting.
  Keep your day solemn. Farewell, I disturb it not;
  I'll bear the smart with patience for a time.

  Exit.

ALSEMERO. 'Tis somewhat ominous this, a quarrel enter'd
  Upon this day. My innocence relieves me,
  I should be wondrous sad else.

  Enter JASPERINO.   80

                        Jasperino,
  I have news to tell thee, strange news.

JASPERINO.   I ha' some too,
  I think as strange as yours; would I might keep
  Mine, so my faith and friendship might be kept in't!
  Faith sir, dispense a little with my zeal
  And let it cool in this.

ALSEMERO.   This puts me on
  And blames thee for thy slowness.

JASPERINO.   All may prove nothing;
  Only a friendly fear that leapt from me, sir.

ALSEMERO. No question it may prove nothing; let's partake
    it, though.

JASPERINO. 'Twas Diaphanta's chance (for to that wench
  I pretend honest love, and she deserves it)   90
  To leave me in a back part of the house,
  A place we chose for private conference;
  She was no sooner gone, but instantly
  I heard your bride's voice in the next room to me,
  And lending more attention, found De Flores
  Louder than she.

ALSEMERO.   De Flores? Thou art out now.

JASPERINO. You'll tell me more anon.

ALSEMERO.   Still I'll prevent thee:
  The very sight of him is poison to her.

JASPERINO. That made me stagger too, but Diaphanta
  At her return confirm'd it.

ALSEMERO.   Diaphanta!   100

JASPERINO. Then fell we both to listen, and words pass'd
  Like those that challenge interest in a woman.

ALSEMERO. Peace, quench thy zeal; 'tis dangerous to thy
     bosom.

JASPERINO. Then truth is full of peril.

ALSEMERO.   Such truths are –
     O were she the sole glory of the earth,
     Had eyes that could shoot fire into kings' breasts,
     And touch'd, she sleeps not here! Yet I have time,
     Though night be near, to be resolv'd hereof,
     And prithee do not weigh me by my passions.

JASPERINO. I never weigh'd friend so.

ALSEMERO.   Done charitably.   110

     [*Gives key.*]

     That key will lead thee to a pretty secret,
     By a Chaldean taught me, and I've [made]
     My study upon some. Bring from my closet
     A glass inscrib'd there with the letter M.
     And question not my purpose.

JASPERINO.   It shall be done, sir.

     Exit.

ALSEMERO. How can this hang together? Not an hour since,
     Her woman came pleading her lady's fears,
     Deliver'd her for the most timorous virgin
     That ever shrunk at man's name, and so modest,
     She charg'd her weep out her request to me,   120
     That she might come obscurely to my bosom.

     Enter BEATRICE.

BEATRICE [*aside*]. All things go well. My woman's preparing
     yonder

For her sweet voyage, which grieves me to lose;
Necessity compels it, I lose all else.

ALSEMERO [*aside*]. Push, modesty's shrine is set in yonder
    forehead.
I cannot be too sure though. – My Joanna!

BEATRICE. Sir, I was bold to weep a message to you;
Pardon my modest fears.

ALSEMERO [*aside*].   The dove's not meeker;
She's abus'd, questionless. –

Enter JASPERINO [*with glass*].

                    O are you come, sir?   130

BEATRICE [*aside*]. The glass, upon my life! I see the letter.

JASPERINO. Sir, this is M.

ALSEMERO.   'Tis it.

BEATRICE [*aside*].   I am suspected.

ALSEMERO. How fitly our bride comes to partake with us!

BEATRICE. What is't, my lord?

ALSEMERO.   No hurt.

BEATRICE.   Sir, pardon me,
I seldom taste of any composition.

ALSEMERO. But this, upon my warrant, you shall venture on.

BEATRICE. I fear 'twill make me ill.

ALSEMERO.   Heaven forbid that.

BEATRICE [*aside*]. I'm put now to my cunning; th'effects I know,
If I can now but feign 'em handsomely.

[Drinks.]

ALSEMERO [*to* JASPERINO]. It has that secret virtue, it ne'er
    miss'd, sir,
Upon a virgin.   140

JASPERINO.   Treble qualitied?

[BEATRICE *gapes, then sneezes.*]

ALSEMERO. By all that's virtuous, it takes there, proceeds!

JASPERINO. This is the strangest trick to know a maid by.

BEATRICE. Ha, ha, ha!
    You have given me joy of heart to drink, my lord.

ALSEMERO. No, thou hast given me such joy of heart,
    That never can be blasted.

BEATRICE.   What's the matter, sir?

ALSEMERO [*to* JASPERINO]. See, now 'tis settled in a
    melancholy.
Keep both the time and method, my Joanna!
Chaste as the breath of heaven, or morning's womb,
That brings the day forth, thus my love encloses thee.   150

[Embraces her.] Exeunt.

[Scene iii]

Enter ISABELLA *and* LOLLIO.

ISABELLA. O heaven! Is this the waiting moon?
    Does love turn fool, run mad, and all [at] once?
    Sirrah, here's a madman, akin to the fool too,

A lunatic lover.

LOLLIO. No, no, not he I brought the letter from?

ISABELLA. Compare his inside with his out, and tell me.

[*Gives him letter.*]

LOLLIO. The out's mad, I'm sure of that; I had a taste on't.
[*Reads.*] 'To the bright Andromeda, chief chambermaid to
the Knight of the Sun, at the sign of Scorpio, in the middle
region, sent by the bellows mender of Aeolus. Pay the post.'
This is stark madness.   10

ISABELLA. Now mark the inside. [*Takes letter and reads.*]
'Sweet lady, having now cast off this counterfeit cover of a
madman, I appear to your best judgment a true and faithful
lover of your beauty.'

LOLLIO. He is mad still.

ISABELLA. 'If any fault you find, chide those perfections in
you, which have made me imperfect; 'tis the same sun that
causeth to grow and enforceth to wither . . . '

LOLLIO. O rogue!

ISABELLA. ' . . . Shapes and trans-shapes, destroys and builds
again; I come in winter to you dismantled of my proper
ornaments; by the sweet splendour of your cheerful smiles,
I spring and live a lover.'

LOLLIO. Mad rascal still!

ISABELLA. 'Tread him not under foot, that shall appear an
honour to your bounties. I remain – mad till I speak with
you, from whom I expect my cure. Yours all, or one beside
himself, *Franciscus*.'

LOLLIO. You are like to have a fine time on't; my master and

I may give over our professions: I do not think but you can
cure fools and madmen faster than we, with little pains too.

ISABELLA. Very likely.   30

LOLLIO. One thing I must tell you, mistress: you perceive
  that I am privy to your skill; if I find you minister once
  and set up the trade, I put in for my thirds, I shall be
  mad or fool else.

ISABELLA. The first place is thine, believe it, Lollio,
  If I do fall –

LOLLIO.   I fall upon you.

ISABELLA.   So.

LOLLIO. Well, I stand to my venture.

ISABELLA. But thy counsel now, how shall I deal with 'em?

LOLLIO. Why, do you mean to deal with 'em?

ISABELLA. Nay, the fair understanding, how to use 'em.

LOLLIO. Abuse 'em! That's the way to mad the fool, and
  make a fool of the madman, and then you use 'em kindly.

ISABELLA. 'Tis easy, I'll practise; do thou observe it;
  The key of thy wardrobe.

LOLLIO. There; fit yourself for 'em, and I'll fit 'em both for you.

  [*Gives her key.*]

ISABELLA. Take thou no further notice than the outside.

  Exit.

LOLLIO. Not an inch; I'll put you to the inside.

  Enter ALIBIUS.

ALIBIUS. Lollio, art there? Will all be perfect, think'st thou?
    Tomorrow night, as if to close up the solemnity,
    Vermandero expects us.

LOLLIO. I mistrust the madmen most; the fools will do well
    enough; I have taken pains with them.

ALIBIUS. Tush, they cannot miss; the more absurdity
    The more commends it, so no rough behaviours
    Affright the ladies; they are nice things, thou know'st.

LOLLIO. You need not fear, sir; so long as we are there with
    our commanding pizzles, they'll be as tame as the ladies
    themselves.

ALIBIUS. I will see them once more rehearse before they go.

LOLLIO. I was about it, sir; look you to the madmen's morris,
    and let me alone with the other; there is one or two that I
    mistrust their fooling; I'll instruct them, and then they shall
    rehearse the whole measure.

ALIBIUS. Do so; I'll see the music prepar'd. But Lollio,   60
    By the way, how does my wife brook her restraint?
    Does she not grudge at it?

LOLLIO. So, so; she takes some pleasure in the house, she
    would abroad else; you must allow her a little more length,
    she's kept too short.

ALIBIUS. She shall along to Vermandero's with us;
    That will serve her for a month's liberty.

LOLLIO. What's that on your face, sir?

ALIBIUS. Where, Lollio? I see nothing.

LOLLIO. Cry you mercy, sir, 'tis your nose; it show'd like the
    trunk of a young elephant.   70

ALIBIUS. Away, rascal! I'll prepare the music, Lollio.

Exit ALIBIUS.

LOLLIO. Do, sir, and I'll dance the whilst. Tony, where art thou, Tony?

Enter ANTONIO.

ANTONIO. Here cousin; where art thou?

LOLLIO. Come, Tony, the footmanship I taught you.

ANTONIO. I had rather ride, cousin.

LOLLIO. Ay, a whip take you; but I'll keep you out. Vault in; look you, Tony: fa, la la, la la.

[*Dances.*]

ANTONIO. Fa, la la, la la.

[*Dances.*]

LOLLIO. There, an honour.

ANTONIO. Is this an honour, cuz?   80

[*Bows.*]

LOLLIO. Yes, and it please your worship.

ANTONIO. Does honour bend in the hams, cuz?

LOLLIO. Marry does it; as low as worship, squireship, nay, yeomanry itself sometimes, from whence it first stiffened; there rise, a caper.

ANTONIO. Caper after an honour, cuz?

LOLLIO. Very proper; for honour is but a caper, rises as fast and high, has a knee or two, and falls to th'ground again. You can remember your figure, Tony?

Exit.

ANTONIO. Yes, cousin; when I see thy figure, I can remember
    mine.

Enter ISABELLA [*disguised as a madwoman*].   90

ISABELLA. Hey, how he treads the air! Shough, shough,
    tother way! He burns his wings else; here's wax enough
    below, Icarus, more than will be cancelled these eighteen
    moons;

He's down, he's down, what a terrible fall he had!
Stand up, thou son of Cretan Dedalus,
And let us tread the lower labyrinth;
I'll bring thee to the clue.

ANTONIO. Prithee, cuz, let me alone.

ISABELLA. Art thou not drown'd?
About thy head I saw a heap of clouds,   100
Wrapp'd like a Turkish turban; on thy back
A crook'd chameleon-colour'd rainbow hung
Like a tiara down unto thy hams.
Let me suck out those billows in thy belly;
Hark how they roar and rumble in the straits!
Bless thee from the pirates.

ANTONIO. Pox upon you, let me alone!

ISABELLA. Why shouldst thou mount so high as Mercury,
Unless thou hadst reversion of his place?
Stay in the moon with me, Endymion,   110
And we will rule these wild rebellious waves
That would have drown'd my love.

ANTONIO. I'll kick thee if again thou touch me,
Thou wild unshapen antic; I am no fool,
You bedlam!

ISABELLA.   But you are, as sure as I am, mad.
  Have I put on this habit of a frantic,
  With love as full of fury, to beguile
  The nimble eye of watchful jealousy,
  And am I thus rewarded?

  [*Reveals herself.*]

ANTONIO. Ha! Dearest beauty!

ISABELLA.   No, I have no beauty now,
  Nor never had, but what was in my garments.   120
  You a quick-sighted lover? Come not near me!
  Keep your caparisons, y'are aptly clad;
  I came a feigner to return stark mad.

  Exit.

  Enter LOLLIO.

ANTONIO. Stay, or I shall change condition,
  And become as you are.

LOLLIO. Why, Tony, whither now? Why, fool?

ANTONIO. Whose fool, usher of idiots? You coxcomb!
  I have fool'd too much.

LOLLIO. You were best be mad another while then.

ANTONIO. So I am, stark mad, I have cause enough;   130
  And I could throw the full effects on thee
  And beat thee like a fury!

LOLLIO. Do not, do not; I shall not forbear the gentleman
  under the fool, if you do; alas, I saw through your fox-skin
  before now. Come, I can give you comfort; my mistress
  loves you, and there is as arrant a madman i' th'house as
  you are a fool, your rival, whom she loves not; if after the

masque we can rid her of him, you earn her love, she says, and the fool shall ride her.

ANTONIO. May I believe thee?

LOLLIO. Yes, or you may choose whether you will or no.   140

ANTONIO. She's eas'd of him; I have a good quarrel on't.

LOLLIO. Well, keep your old station yet, and be quiet.

ANTONIO. Tell her I will deserve her love.

[*Exit.*]

LOLLIO. And you are like to have your desire.

Enter FRANCISCUS.

FRANCISCUS (*sings*).
  '*Down, down, down a-down a-down*',
  And then with a horse-trick,
  To kick Latona's forehead, and break her bowstring.

LOLLIO [*aside*]. This is tother counterfeit; I'll put him out of his humour. [*Takes out letter and reads.*] 'Sweet lady, having now cast this counterfeit cover of a madman, I appear to your best judgment a true and faithful lover of your beauty.' This is pretty well for a madman.

FRANCISCUS. Ha! What's that?

LOLLIO. 'Chide those perfections in you, which made me imperfect.'

FRANCISCUS. I am discover'd to the fool.

LOLLIO. I hope to discover the fool in you, ere I have done with you. 'Yours all, or one beside himself, *Franciscus*.' This madman will mend sure.

FRANCISCUS. What? Do you read, sirrah?   160

LOLLIO. Your destiny, sir; you'll be hang'd for this trick, and
    another that I know.

FRANCISCUS. Art thou of counsel with thy mistress?

LOLLIO. Next her apron strings.

FRANCISCUS. Give me thy hand.

LOLLIO. Stay, let me put yours in my pocket first. [*Puts away
    letter.*] Your hand is true, is it not? It will not pick? I partly
    fear it, because I think it does lie.

FRANCISCUS. Not in a syllable.

LOLLIO. So; if you love my mistress so well as you have
    handled the matter here, you are like to be cur'd of your
    madness.

FRANCISCUS. And none but she can cure it.

LOLLIO. Well, I'll give you over then, and she shall cast your
    water next.

FRANCISCUS. Take for thy pains past.

    [*Gives him money.*]

LOLLIO. I shall deserve more, sir, I hope; my mistress loves
    you, but must have some proof of your love to her.

FRANCISCUS. There I meet my wishes.

LOLLIO. That will not serve, you must meet her enemy and
    yours.

FRANCISCUS. He's dead already!   180

LOLLIO. Will you tell me that, and I parted but now with him?

FRANCISCUS. Show me the man.

LOLLIO. Ay, that's a right course now, see him before you kill him in any case, and yet it needs not go so far neither; 'tis but a fool that haunts the house and my mistress in the shape of an idiot; hang but his fool's coat well-flavouredly, and 'tis well.

FRANCISCUS. Soundly, soundly!

LOLLIO. Only reserve him till the masque be past, and if you find him not now in the dance yourself, I'll show you. In, in! My master!

FRANCISCUS. He handles him like a feather. Hey!

[*Exit dancing.*]   190

Enter ALIBIUS.

ALIBIUS. Well said; in a readiness, Lollio?

LOLLIO. Yes, sir.

ALIBIUS. Away then, and guide them in, Lollio;
Entreat your mistress to see this sight.
Hark, is there not one incurable fool
That might be begg'd? I have friends.

LOLLIO [*within*]. I have him for you, one that shall deserve it too.

[*Exit* LOLLIO.]

ALIBIUS. Good boy, Lollio.   200

[*Enter* ISABELLA, *then* LOLLIO *with* MADMEN *and* FOOLS.] *The* MADMEN *and* FOOLS *dance.*

'Tis perfect; well, fit but once these strains,
We shall have coin and credit for our pains.

Exeunt.

ACT FIVE

[Scene i]

Enter BEATRICE. *A clock strikes one.*

BEATRICE. One struck, and yet she lies by't – O my fears!
　　This strumpet serves her own ends, 'tis apparent now,
　　Devours the pleasure with a greedy appetite,
　　And never minds my honour or my peace,
　　Makes havoc of my right; but she pays dearly for't:
　　No trusting of her life with such a secret,
　　That cannot rule her blood to keep her promise.
　　Beside, I have some suspicion of her faith to me
　　Because I was suspected of my lord,
　　And it must come from her. – Hark! By my horrors,　　10
　　Another clock strikes two.

　　Strikes two.

　　Enter DE FLORES.

DE FLORES.　　　　　　Pist, where are you?

BEATRICE. De Flores?

DE FLORES.　　　　　Ay – Is she not come from him yet?

BEATRICE. As I am a living soul, not.

DE FLORES.　　　　　　　　　Sure the Devil
　　Hath sow'd his itch within her; who'd trust
　　A waiting-woman?

BEATRICE.　　　I must trust somebody.

DE FLORES. Push, they are termagants,
    Especially when they fall upon their masters
    And have their ladies' first-fruits; th'are mad whelps,
    You cannot stave 'em off from game royal; then   20
    You are so harsh and hardy, ask no counsel,
    And I could have help'd you to an apothecary's daughter
    Would have fall'n off before eleven, and thank you too.

BEATRICE. O me, not yet? This whore forgets herself.

DE FLORES. The rascal fares so well; look, y'are undone,
    The day-star, by this hand! See Phosphorus plain yonder.

BEATRICE. Advise me now to fall upon some ruin,
    There is no counsel safe else.

DE FLORES.   Peace, I ha't now;
    For we must force a rising, there's no remedy.

BEATRICE. How? Take heed of that.

DE FLORES.   Tush, be you quiet,
    Or else give over all.

BEATRICE.   Prithee, I ha' done then.   30

DE FLORES. This is my reach: I'll set some part a-fire
    Of Diaphanta's chamber.

BEATRICE.   How? Fire, sir?
    That may endanger the whole house.

DE FLORES. You talk of danger when your fame's on fire?

BEATRICE. That's true; do what thou wilt now.

DE FLORES.   Push, I aim
    At a most rich success, strikes all dead sure;
    The chimney being a-fire, and some light parcels
    Of the least danger in her chamber only,

If Diaphanta should be met by chance then,
Far from her lodging, which is now suspicious,   40
It would be thought her fears and affrights then
Drove her to seek for succour; if not seen
Or met at all, as that's the likeliest,
For her own shame she'll hasten towards her lodging;
I will be ready with a piece high-charg'd,
As 'twere to cleanse the chimney: there 'tis proper now,
But she shall be the mark.

BEATRICE.   I'm forc'd to love thee now,
'Cause thou provid'st so carefully for my honour.

DE FLORES: 'Slid, it concerns the safety of us both,
Our pleasure and continuance.   50

BEATRICE.   One word now, prithee;
How for the servants?

DE FLORES.   I'll dispatch them
Some one way, some another in the hurry,
For buckets, hooks, ladders. Fear not you;
The deed shall find its time – and I've thought since
Upon a safe conveyance for the body too.
How this fire purifies wit! Watch you your minute.

BEATRICE. Fear keeps my soul upon't, I cannot stray from't.

Enter ALONZO'S GHOST.

DE FLORES. Ha! What art thou that tak'st away the light
'Twixt that star and me? I dread thee not;   60
'Twas but a mist of conscience – all's clear again.

Exit.

BEATRICE. Who's that, De Flores? Bless me! It slides by;

[*Exit* GHOST.]

Some ill thing haunts the house; 't has left behind it
A shivering sweat upon me; I'm afraid now,
This night hath been so tedious. O this strumpet!
Had she a thousand lives, he should not leave her
Till he had destroy'd the last – List, O my terrors!

Struck three o'clock.

Three struck by Saint Sebastian's!

[VOICE] (*within*).   Fire, fire, fire!

BEATRICE. Already? How rare is that man's speed!
  How heartily he serves me! His face loathes one,   70
  But look upon his care, who would not love him?
  The east is not more beauteous than his service.

[VOICE] (*within*). Fire, fire, fire!

Enter DE FLORES; SERVANTS *pass over, ring a bell.*

DE FLORES.   Away, dispatch!
  Hooks, buckets, ladders! That's well said;
  The fire-bell rings, the chimney works; my charge;
  The piece is ready.

  Exit.

BEATRICE.   Here's a man worth loving –

Enter DIAPHANTA.

  O y'are a jewel!

DIAPHANTA.   Pardon frailty, madam;
  In troth I was so well, I ev'n forgot myself.

BEATRICE. Y'have made trim work.

DIAPHANTA.   What?

BEATRICE.   Hie quickly to your chamber;
  Your reward follows you.

DIAPHANTA.   I never made
  So sweet a bargain.

  Exit.

  Enter ALSEMERO.

ALSEMERO.   O my dear Joanna;   80
  Alas, art thou risen too? I was coming,
  My absolute treasure.

BEATRICE.   When I miss'd you,
  I could not choose but follow.

ALSEMERO.   Th'art all sweetness!
  The fire is not so dangerous.

BEATRICE.   Think you so, sir?

ALSEMERO. I prithee tremble not: believe me, 'tis not.

  Enter VERMANDERO, JASPERINO.

VERMANDERO. O bless my house and me!

ALSEMERO.   My lord your father.

  Enter DE FLORES *with a piece.*

VERMANDERO. Knave, whither goes that piece?

DE FLORES.   To scour the chimney.

  Exit.

VERMANDERO. O well said, well said;
  That fellow's good on all occasions.

BEATRICE. A wondrous necessary man, my lord.   90

VERMANDERO. He hath a ready wit, he's worth 'em all, sir;
    Dog at a house of fire; I ha' seen him sing'd ere now:

The piece goes off.

    Ha, there he goes.

BEATRICE.   'Tis done.

ALSEMERO.   Come, sweet, to bed now;
    Alas, thou wilt get cold.

BEATRICE.   Alas, the fear keeps that out;
    My heart will find no quiet till I hear
    How Diaphanta, my poor woman, fares;
    It is her chamber, sir, her lodging chamber.

VERMANDERO. How should the fire come there?

BEATRICE. As good a soul as ever lady countenanc'd,
    But in her chamber negligent and heavy;   100
    She 'scap'd a mine twice.

VERMANDERO.   Twice?

BEATRICE.   Strangely twice, sir.

VERMANDERO. Those sleepy sluts are dangerous in a house
    And they be ne'er so good.

Enter DE FLORES.

DE FLORES.   O poor virginity!
    Thou hast paid dearly for't.

VERMANDERO.   Bless us! What's that?

DE FLORES. A thing you all knew once; Diaphanta's burnt.

BEATRICE. My woman, O, my woman!

DE FLORES.   Now the flames

Are greedy of her; burnt, burnt, burnt to death, sir!

BEATRICE. O my presaging soul!

ALSEMERO.   Not a tear more;
  I charge you by the last embrace I gave you
  In bed before this rais'd us.   110

BEATRICE.   Now you tie me;
  Were it my sister, now she gets no more.

  Enter SERVANT.

VERMANDERO. How now?

SERVANT. All danger's past, you may now take your rests, my
  lords; the fire is throughly quench'd; ah, poor gentlewoman,
  how soon was she stifled!

BEATRICE. De Flores, what is left of her inter,
  And we as mourners all will follow her:
  I will entreat that honour to my servant,
  Ev'n of my lord himself.

ALSEMERO.   Command it, sweetness.

BEATRICE. Which of you spied the fire first?   120

DE FLORES.   'Twas I, madam.

BEATRICE. And took such pains in't too? A double goodness!
  'Twere well he were rewarded.

VERMANDERO.   He shall be;
  De Flores, call upon me.

ALSEMERO.   And upon me, sir.

  Exeunt [all but DE FLORES].

DE FLORES. Rewarded? Precious, here's a trick beyond me!

I see in all bouts, both of sport and wit,
Always a woman strives for the last hit.

Exit.

[Scene ii]

Enter TOMAZO.

TOMAZO. I cannot taste the benefits of life
    With the same relish I was wont to do.
    Man I grow weary of, and hold his fellowship
    A treacherous bloody friendship; and because
    I am ignorant in whom my wrath should settle,
    I must think all men villains, and the next
    I meet, whoe'er he be, the murderer
    Of my most worthy brother. – Ha! What's he?

Enter DE FLORES, *passes over the stage.*

    O the fellow that some call honest De Flores;
    But methinks honesty was hard bested   10
    To come there for a lodging, as if a queen
    Should make her palace of a pest-house.
    I find a contrariety in nature
    Betwixt that face and me: the least occasion
    Would give me game upon him; yet he's so foul,
    One would scarce touch [him] with a sword he loved
    And made account of; so most deadly venomous,
    He would go near to poison any weapon
    That should draw blood on him; one must resolve
    Never to use that sword again in fight,   20
    In way of honest manhood, that strikes him;
    Some river must devour't, 'twere not fit

That any man should find it. – What, again?

Enter DE FLORES.

He walks a' purpose by, sure, to choke me up,
To infect my blood.

DE FLORES.   My worthy noble lord!

TOMAZO. Dost offer to come near and breathe upon me?

[*Strikes him.*]

DE FLORES. A blow!

[*Draws sword.*]

TOMAZO.   Yea, are you so prepar'd?
I'll rather like a soldier die by th'sword
Than like a politician by thy poison.

[*Draws.*]   30

DE FLORES. Hold, my lord, as you are honourable.

TOMAZO. All slaves that kill by poison are still cowards.

DE FLORES [*aside*]. I cannot strike; I see his brother's wounds
Fresh bleeding in his eye, as in a crystal.
I will not question this, I know y'are noble.
I take my injury with thanks given, sir,
Like a wise lawyer; and as a favour,
Will wear it for the worthy hand that gave it.
[*Aside.*] Why this from him, that yesterday appear'd
So strangely loving to me?   40
O but instinct is of a subtler strain,
Guilt must not walk so near his lodge again;
He came near me now.

Exit.

TOMAZO. All league with mankind I renounce for ever
   Till I find this murderer; not so much
   As common courtesy but I'll lock up:
   For in the state of ignorance I live in,
   A brother may salute his brother's murderer
   And wish good speed to th'villain in a greeting.

Enter VERMANDERO, ALIBIUS *and* ISABELLA.

VERMANDERO. Noble Piracquo!

TOMAZO.   Pray keep on your way, sir,
   I've nothing to say to you.   50

VERMANDERO.   Comforts bless you, sir.

TOMAZO. I have forsworn compliment; in troth I have, sir;
   As you are merely man, I have not left
   A good wish for you, nor any here.

VERMANDERO. Unless you be so far in love with grief
   You will not part from't upon any terms,
   We bring that news will make a welcome for us.

TOMAZO. What news can that be?

VERMANDERO.   Throw no scornful smile
   Upon the zeal I bring you, 'tis worth more, sir.
   Two of the chiefest men I kept about me
   I hide not from the law, or your just vengeance.   60

TOMAZO. Ha!

VERMANDERO. To give your peace more ample satisfaction,
   Thank these discoverers.

TOMAZO.   If you bring that calm,
   Name but the manner I shall ask forgiveness in
   For that contemptuous smile upon you:

I'll perfect it with reverence that belongs
Unto a sacred altar.

[*Kneels.*]

VERMANDERO.   Good sir, rise;
Why, now you overdo as much a'this hand,
As you fell short a' tother. Speak, Alibius.

ALIBIUS. 'Twas my wife's fortune, as she is most lucky   70
At a discovery, to find out lately
Within our hospital of fools and madmen
Two counterfeits slipp'd into these disguises:
Their names, Franciscus and Antonio.

VERMANDERO. Both mine, sir, and I ask no favour for 'em.

ALIBIUS. Now that which draws suspicion to their habits,
The time of their disguisings agrees justly
With the day of the murder.

TOMAZO.   O blest revelation!

VERMANDERO. Nay more, nay more, sir, I'll not spare
      mine own
In way of justice: they both feign'd a journey   80
To Briamata, and so wrought out their leaves;
My love was so abus'd in't.

TOMAZO.   Time's too precious
To run in waste now; you have brought a peace
The riches of five kingdoms could not purchase.
Be my most happy conduct; I thirst for 'em:
Like subtle lightning will I wind about 'em,
And melt their marrow in 'em.

Exeunt.

[Scene iii]

Enter ALSEMERO *and* JASPERINO.

JASPERINO. Your confidence, I'm sure, is now of proof.
  The prospect from the garden has show'd
  Enough for deep suspicion.

ALSEMERO.   The black mask
  That so continually was worn upon't
  Condemns the face for ugly ere't be seen:
  Her despite to him, and so seeming bottomless.

JASPERINO. Touch it home then; 'tis not a shallow probe
  Can search this ulcer soundly; I fear you'll find it
  Full of corruption. 'Tis fit I leave you;   10
  She meets you opportunely from that walk:
  She took the back door at his parting with her.

  Exit JASPERINO.

ALSEMERO. Did my fate wait for this unhappy stroke
  At my first sight of woman? – She's here.

  Enter BEATRICE.

BEATRICE. Alsemero!

ALSEMERO.   How do you?

BEATRICE.   How do I?
  Alas! How do you? You look not well.

ALSEMERO. You read me well enough, I am not well.

BEATRICE. Not well, sir? Is't in my power to better you?

ALSEMERO. Yes.

BEATRICE.   Nay, then y'are cur'd again.

ALSEMERO. Pray resolve me one question, lady.

BEATRICE.   If I can.   20

ALSEMERO. None can so sure. Are you honest?

BEATRICE. Ha, ha, ha! That's a broad question, my lord.

ALSEMERO. But that's not a modest answer, my lady.
  Do you laugh? My doubts are strong upon me.

BEATRICE. 'Tis innocence that smiles, and no rough brow
  Can take away the dimple in her cheek.
  Say I should strain a tear to fill the vault,
  Which would you give the better faith to?

ALSEMERO. 'Twere but hypocrisy of a sadder colour,
  But the same stuff; neither your smiles nor tears
  Shall move or flatter me from my belief.   30
  You are a whore!

BEATRICE.   What a horrid sound it hath!
  It blasts a beauty to deformity;
  Upon what face soever that breath falls,
  It strikes it ugly. O you have ruin'd
  What you can ne'er repair again.

ALSEMERO. I'll all demolish, and seek out truth within you,
  If there be any left; let your sweet tongue
  Prevent your heart's rifling; there I'll ransack
  And tear out my suspicion.

BEATRICE.   You may, sir,
  'Tis an easy passage; yet, if you please,   40
  Show me the ground whereon you lost your love;
  My spotless virtue may but tread on that
  Before I perish.

ALSEMERO.   Unanswerable!
  A ground you cannot stand on: you fall down
  Beneath all grace and goodness, when you set
  Your ticklish heel on't; there was a visor
  O'er that cunning face, and that became you;
  Now impudence in triumph rides upon't.
  How comes this tender reconcilement else
  'Twixt you and your despite, your rancorous loathing,   50
  De Flores? He that your eye was sore at sight of,
  He's now become your arm's supporter, your lip's saint!

BEATRICE. Is there the cause?

ALSEMERO.   Worse: your lust's devil,
  Your adultery!

BEATRICE.   Would any but yourself say that,
  'Twould turn him to a villain.

ALSEMERO.   'Twas witness'd
  By the counsel of your bosom, Diaphanta.

BEATRICE. Is your witness dead then?

ALSEMERO.   'Tis to be fear'd
  It was the wages of her knowledge, poor soul,
  She liv'd not long after the discovery.

BEATRICE. Then hear a story of not much less horror   60
  Than this your false suspicion is beguil'd with;
  To your bed's scandal I stand up innocence,
  Which even the guilt of one black other deed
  Will stand for proof of: your love has made me
  A cruel murd'ress.

ALSEMERO.   Ha!

BEATRICE.   A bloody one.
  I have kiss'd poison for't, strok'd a serpent:

That thing of hate, worthy in my esteem
Of no better employment, and him most worthy
To be so employ'd, I caus'd to murder   70
That innocent Piracquo, having no
Better means than that worst, to assure
Yourself to me.

ALSEMERO.   O the place itself e'er since
Has crying been for vengeance, the temple
Where blood and beauty first unlawfully
Fir'd their devotion, and quench'd the right one;
'Twas in my fears at first, 'twill have it now:
O thou art all deform'd!

BEATRICE.   Forget not, sir,
It for your sake was done; shall greater dangers
Make the less welcome?

ALSEMERO.   O thou shouldst have gone   80
A thousand leagues about to have avoided
This dangerous bridge of blood; here we are lost.

BEATRICE. Remember I am true unto your bed.

ALSEMERO. The bed itself's a charnel, the sheets shrouds
For murdered carcasses; it must ask pause
What I must do in this; meantime you shall
Be my prisoner only: enter my closet;

Exit BEATRICE.

I'll be your keeper yet. O in what part
Of this sad story shall I first begin? – Ha!

Enter DE FLORES.

This same fellow has put me in – De Flores!

DE FLORES. Noble Alsemero?   90

ALSEMERO.   I can tell you
  News, sir; my wife has her commended to you.

DE FLORES. That's news indeed, my lord; I think she would
  Commend me to the gallows if she could,
  She ever lov'd me so well; I thank her.

ALSEMERO. What's this blood upon your hand, De Flores?

DE FLORES. Blood? No, sure, 'twas wash'd since.

ALSEMERO.   Since when, man?

DE FLORES. Since tother day I got a knock
  In a sword and dagger school; I think 'tis out.

ALSEMERO. Yes, 'tis almost out, but 'tis perceiv'd though.
  I had forgot my message; this it is: 100
  What price goes murder?

DE FLORES.   How, sir?

ALSEMERO.   I ask you, sir;
  My wife's behindhand with you, she tells me,
  For a brave bloody blow you gave for her sake
  Upon Piracquo.

DE FLORES.   Upon? 'Twas quite through him, sure;
  Has she confess'd it?

ALSEMERO.   As sure as death to both of you,
  And much more than that.

DE FLORES.   It could not be much more;
  'Twas but one thing, and that – she's a whore.

ALSEMERO. It could not choose but follow. O cunning devils!
  How should blind men know you from fair-fac'd saints?

BEATRICE (*within*). He lies, the villain does belie me!   110

DE FLORES. Let me go to her, sir.

ALSEMERO.   Nay, you shall to her.
  Peace, crying crocodile, your sounds are heard!
  Take your prey to you, get you in to her, sir.

  Exit DE FLORES.

  I'll be your pander now; rehearse again
  Your scene of lust, that you may be perfect
  When you shall come to act it to the black audience
  Where howls and gnashings shall be music to you.
  Clip your adult'ress freely, 'tis the pilot
  Will guide you to the Mare Mortuum,
  Where you shall sink to fathoms bottomless.   120

  Enter VERMANDERO, ALIBIUS, ISABELLA, TOMAZO,
  FRANCISCUS, *and* ANTONIO.

VERMANDERO. O Alsemero, I have a wonder for you.

ALSEMERO. No, sir, 'tis I, I have a wonder for you.

VERMANDERO. I have suspicion near as proof itself
  For Piracquo's murder.

ALSEMERO.   Sir, I have proof
  Beyond suspicion for Piracquo's murder.

VERMANDERO. Beseech you hear me; these two have been
      disguis'd
  E'er since the deed was done.

ALSEMERO.   I have two other
  That were more close disguis'd than your two could be,
  E'er since the deed was done.   130

VERMANDERO. You'll hear me! These mine own servants –

ALSEMERO. Hear me! Those nearer than your servants,

That shall acquit them and prove them guiltless.

FRANCISCUS. That may be done with easy truth, sir.

TOMAZO. How is my cause bandied through your delays!
    'Tis urgent in blood and calls for haste;
    Give me a brother alive or dead;
    Alive, a wife with him; if dead, for both
    A recompense, for murder and adultery.

BEATRICE (*within*). O! O! O!

ALSEMERO.   Hark, 'tis coming to you.

DE FLORES (*within*). Nay, I'll along for company.   140

BEATRICE (*within*).   O! O!

VERMANDERO. What horrid sounds are these?

ALSEMERO. Come forth, you twins of mischief!

    Enter DE FLORES *bringing in* BEATRICE [*wounded*].

DE FLORES. Here we are; if you have any more
    To say to us, speak quickly; I shall not
    Give you the hearing else; I am so stout yet,
    And so, I think, that broken rib of mankind.

VERMANDERO. An host of enemies enter'd my citadel
    Could not amaze like this: Joanna! Beatrice-Joanna!

BEATRICE. O come not near me, sir, I shall defile you:
    I am that of your blood was taken from you   150
    For your better health; look no more upon't,
    But cast it to the ground regardlessly,
    Let the common sewer take it from distinction.
    Beneath the stars, upon yon meteor
    Ever hung my fate, 'mongst things corruptible;
    I ne'er could pluck it from him: my loathing

Was prophet to the rest, but ne'er believ'd;
Mine honour fell with him, and now my life.
Alsemero, I am a stranger to your bed,
Your bed was cozen'd on the nuptial night,   160
For which your false bride died.

ALSEMERO.   Diaphanta!

DE FLORES. Yes, and the while I coupled with your mate
     At barley-brake; now we are left in hell.

VERMANDERO. We are all there, it circumscribes here.

DE FLORES. I lov'd this woman in spite of her heart;
     Her love I earn'd out of Piracquo's murder.

TOMAZO. Ha! My brother's murderer!

DE FLORES.   Yes, and her honour's prize
     Was my reward; I thank life for nothing
     But that pleasure; it was so sweet to me
     That I have drunk up all, left none behind   170
     For any man to pledge me.

VERMANDERO.   Horrid villain!
     Keep life in him for further tortures.

DE FLORES.   No!
     I can prevent you; here's my penknife still.
     It is but one thread more, [*Stabs himself.*] − and now 'tis cut.
     Make haste, Joanna, by that token to thee:
     Canst not forget, so lately put in mind,
     I would not go to leave thee far behind.

     Dies.

BEATRICE. Forgive me, Alsemero, all forgive;
     'Tis time to die, when 'tis a shame to live.   179

Dies.

VERMANDERO. O my name is enter'd now in that record
 Where till this fatal hour 'twas never read.

ALSEMERO. Let it be blotted out, let your heart lose it,
 And it can never look you in the face,
 Nor tell a tale behind the back of life
 To your dishonour; justice hath so right
 The guilty hit, that innocence is quit
 By proclamation, and may joy again.
 Sir, you are sensible of what truth hath done;
 Tis the best comfort that your grief can find.   190

TOMAZO. Sir, I am satisfied, my injuries
 Lie dead before me; I can exact no more,
 Unless my soul were loose, and could o'ertake
 Those black fugitives that are fled from thence
 To take a second vengeance; but there are wraths
 Deeper than mine, 'tis to be fear'd, about 'em.

ALSEMERO. What an opacous body had that moon
 That last chang'd on us! Here's beauty chang'd
 To ugly whoredom; here, servant obedience
 To a master sin, imperious murder;   200
 I, a suppos'd husband, chang'd embraces
 With wantonness, but that was paid before;
 Your change is come too, from an ignorant wrath
 To knowing friendship. Are there any more on's?

ANTONIO. Yes, sir; I was chang'd too, from a little ass as
 I was to a great fool as I am; and had like to ha' been
 chang'd to the gallows, but that you know my innocence
 always excuses me.

FRANCISCUS. I was chang'd from a little wit to be stark mad,
 Almost for the same purpose.

ISABELLA [*to* ALIBIUS].   Your change is still behind,
　　But deserve best your transformation: 210
　　You are a jealous coxcomb, keep schools of folly,
　　And teach your scholars how to break your own head.

ALIBIUS. I see all apparent, wife, and will change now
　　Into a better husband, and never keep
　　Scholars that shall be wiser than myself.

ALSEMERO. Sir, you have yet a son's duty living,
　　Please you accept it; let that your sorrow,
　　As it goes from your eye, go from your heart;
　　Man and his sorrow at the grave must part.

Epilogue

ALSEMERO. All we can do to comfort one another,
　　To stay a brother's sorrow for a brother,   220
　　To dry a child from the kind father's eyes,
　　Is to no purpose, it rather multiplies:
　　Your only smiles have power to cause relive
　　The dead again, or in their rooms to give
　　Brother a new brother, father a child;
　　If these appear, all griefs are reconcil'd.

Exeunt omnes.

Finis.

Glossary

a'God's name – free

Aeolus – the Greek god of winds

Anacreon – Greek poet supposed to have choked on a grape pip

Andromeda – in Greek mythology, Perseus rescued Andromeda from a dragon

answerable – appropriate

antic – grotesque performer, clown

Ars Amandi – *The Art of Love*, a work by the Roman poet Ovid (43 BC-AD 17)

aunt – prostitute

band – cuff or collar

bankers – people who repaired the banks of rivers or dikes

basilisk – mythical creature that killed by a look

bauble – penis (slang)

beadle – parish official (with connotations of stupidity)

behindhand with – indebted to

Belike – probably

Bucephalus – Alexander the Great's horse; only he could ride it.

buckler – shield

by-bet – side bet

cabinets – safes

caparisons – clothes

capcase – wallet

casement – window

cast – throw of the dice

cast your water – examine your urine in order to diagnose an illness

catch the last couple in hell – a reference to the game of barley-brake, a form of tag in which there is an area called hell, with metaphorical connotations for both Isabella and Beatrice-Joanna

Chaldean – magician

charge – gunpowder

charnel – charnel house, a place where bones are stored

chimes of Bedlam – the cries of madmen asking for food.

Bedlam, meaning 'madhouse', derives from Bethlehem Hospital

clue (4.3) — the thread Ariadne gave to Theseus to help him escape from the labyrinth

commodious — successful

composition — drink of mixed ingredients

conceit — fancy

cousin — relative, sometimes with the sense of whore

cozened — betrayed

cuckoo (what you call't) — wild arum or cuckoo-pintle, a plant of phallic appearance

cuckoo — (3.3) used to suggest Alibius may be about to be cuckolded

Cuds — a mild expletive, derived from 'God's'

Dedalus — the builder of the labyrinth on Crete and father of Icarus

Diomed — mythological king of Thrace who fed his horses on human flesh

Dog at — experienced in dealing with

drawing arctics — i. e. the magnetic pole

Dryades — wood nymphs

Endymion — in Greek mythology, the beloved of the moon goddess

Esculapius — Greek god of medicine

exceptious — prone to object

fag — end

favour — love token

figure — dance steps

folio — page

fox-skin — disguise

frantic — lunatic

Galaxia — the Milky Way

Garden-bull — a bull from Paris Garden, used for baiting

habit — clothes

headborough — petty constable (with connotations of stupidity)

Hecate — goddess of witchcraft, often associated with the moon

Hie — go quickly

honest/y — chaste/chastity

honour — bow

humour — fancy

Icarus — in Greek mythology, the son of Dedalus, who flew too near the sun on wings his father had made out of wax and feathers and was drowned

impudence — lack of modesty

incontinently – at once

instruct two benefices – clergymen sometimes held office in two parishes

Iulan down – the first growth of a beard

journeyman – professional

Juno – the Latin name of the wife of the supreme god Zeus (Latin, Jupiter)

Justice – Justice of the Peace (with connotations of stupidity)

kick the dog…bush – the man in the moon had a dog and carried a bush

Lacedemonian – Spartan, possibly a reference to laconic speech, possibly a reference to Helen (of Troy) with connotations of promiscuity; possibly both.

Latona – the Latin form of the name of the mother of Diana (Greek, Artemis), moon goddess and hunter. Probably means Diana herself rather than her mother here.

laws of the Medes – unalterable laws (proverbial)

Lipsius – Justus Lipsius (1547-1606), a scholar whose name invites a pun on lips

list – listen

Luna – moon

lycanthropi – sufferers from lycanthropia, a disease associated with the moon. They believed they were wolves.

magnifico – someone of great legal authority

Mare Mortuum – the Dead Sea, here seen as the entrance to hell

Mercury – the messenger of the gods

munition – fortifications

murderers – small cannons

nigget – fool

Oberon – king of the fairies, particularly in *A Midsummer Night's Dream*

opacous – opaque, ominous

orchard of the Hesperides – the Hesperides were nymphs who guarded an orchard that grew golden apples

ordnance – artillery

orisons – prayers

Orlando – the hero of the Italian poet Ariosto's *Orlando Furioso* (1532), a belligerent fighter *parcels* – items

parlous – dangerous

permasant – Parmesan cheese

Phosphorus – the Morning-star

physnomy – physiognomy, face

piece – gun

pinfold – animal pen

pit-hole – grave, with erotic connotations

pizzles – whips made from bulls' penises

pluck a rose – urinate

poppy – medicinal preparation from poppies

postern – side door

presaging – prophetic

push-pin – a children's game

put case – suppose

reach – plan

receipts – recipes

refulgent – reflecting

reversion – right to succeed to a position

sconce – fortification

scrutinous – searching

Secrets in Nature – *De Arcanis Naturae* by Antonius Mizaldus (1520-78) does not contain these tests but he includes similar ones in other works

several – different

simple – medicinal herb

'Slid – a mild expletive, formed from 'God's [eye] lid'

sooth – truth

Strangely – miraculously

stultus, stulta, stultum – the male, female and neuter forms of the Latin word for foolish.

sutler – army trader

termagants – fierce women

tiara – a long-tailed headdress

ticklish – lascivious

Tiresias – mythological Greek soothsayer who was a man and a woman at different times in his life. He was blinded by Juno.

Titania – queen of the fairies, particularly in *A Midsummer Night's Dream*

to boot – into the bargain

touch'd – tainted

toy – silly notion

turtle – turtle dove

vault – heaven

victuals – food and drink

ward (1.2.61) – defence

wild-geese – prostitutes

wire – whip

withal – as well

worm – conscience